MW01716513

KTOWN

The Foundation and Resilience of Growth

By Faithe Penn

Table Of Contents

Dedication

For Mama and Ray

Introduction

Memory is a thin thread that ties us to the past, tying together the events, people, and locations that have influenced who we are. In my 53 years of existence, I've experienced nearly every conceivable phase of life and encountered numerous hardships, setbacks, and failures. However, these challenges have imparted a crucial lesson: there's wisdom to be gained from adversity, to learn something from them. The difficulties I faced weren't entirely negative; they provided me with insights that no institution could ever offer.

This book is an exploration of those experiences, reliving the love, laughter, and teachings that shaped my life. Every chapter is a meaningful piece of my past. Every encounter influenced how I perceived the world and my role in it. I want to share a valuable lesson that life has taught me with everyone out there. This isn't just an autobiography; it's meant to inspire those who are struggling with similar challenges and feeling defeated. If you think that bad things only happen to you and that life is unfair solely to you, remember that life can be tough for everyone.

There are moments when it seems like life is particularly harsh, especially when you compare yourself to others who seem to have it better. You might find yourself blaming past choices or current situations for your struggles. This book is dedicated to those individuals, offering a reality check that life is unfair to everyone. Yet, there's another perspective that people often forget to consider: every challenge you face carries a lesson. These hardships make you wiser and shape your perspective toward life and the world. It teaches you how to come back in life, how to fight, how to hustle, and how to win. Without facing these obstacles, you may never truly grasp the essence of life.

In sharing these memories, I have chosen to alter some names of those who played a significant part in my story to symbolic names with a twist to enhance their character. I want to focus on the moral of the story and not on the individual. This relays the spirit of their impact and respects their private lives.

This book is not just a recollection of events but a celebration of discovery—of home, of friendship, and of myself. It is a tribute to the resilience of the human spirit and the power of connection. Come along with me into the stories that shaped my path.

One

The Light of Discovery

When I reminisced about my childhood, I always pictured myself standing in front of the apartment where I believed I had come after birth. I entered this world surrounded by my mother's love, but in my adulthood, I learned that the place that I always considered "home" wasn't the place where I spent my initial days. The early days of my life were spent in a different part of the neighborhood, one that I wouldn't remember.

When I was 3 years old, my mother moved to a new place that later became my "home," the most familiar of all—4417B 9th Terrace North in Kingston Projects, Birmingham, Alabama. It was the address I held in my mind for decades. A place where I thought my earliest memories were made. It wasn't until my late twenties, when Mama finally moved out of that apartment, that I learned the truth.

At 53, as I sat on my bed, an ordinary day transformed into something new. Papers were scattered all over the place similar to the chaos in my mind. I looked at my birth certificate, aided by the sunlight shining through the window. Suddenly, I made a discovery that changed my entire perspective: my story didn't begin at 4417B 9th Terrace North in Kingston; instead, it started at 4516 Apt C, 9th Avenue North in Kingston.

For years, my siblings had told me we lived at a different address during my early childhood, but I denied it because I couldn't remember. As I thought about my past now, I began to realize that my memories and imagination had intertwined in those early years, making me feel as though I was in an unfamiliar world. Yet, as I stopped for a moment and meditated on the pieces of those memories, they slowly began to fall into place.

I could vividly recall playing in an apartment that felt like a dream, only to realize now that it wasn't just an imagined vision. It was my very own childhood home until I turned three. In that space, the room was filled with old furniture, much like the ones in the old photographs. The memories controlled my mind, indulging me in the story of my family and neighborhood.

As I traced the address on the paper with my finger, my heart sank. With each passing second, both surprise and clarity washed over me. *I had been wrong all this time*. The story of my life didn't begin where I had always thought; it started in that smaller apartment, filled with love and surrounded by family. My grandmother's apartment was just behind ours.

Suddenly, my mind shifted to the past, and my age seemed to fade away. I was no longer a fifty-three-year-old woman burdened with memories; I was a child again—a young Faithe joyfully running through the small apartment. Though the walls may have felt tight, I remember the laughter that poured from my mouth, filling every corner of that happy space.

"Nobody can catch me! I can run fast!" I giggled, darting in and out between the old furniture. My world was full of joy, innocence, and freedom. I whisked around the gentle silhouettes of the adults', their faces warm with love and protection, gracing me with a sense of safety and security.

I rushed into the kitchen with a flash of energy and caught a glimpse of my mother watching me from the shadows. Her beautiful smile wrapped around my heart with warmth, but just as quickly, the memory faded, leaving me both comforted and longing for more.

As I returned to the present, the pieces of home began to align. This memory helped me uncover the truth about my past and allowed me to explore the story of my family and the neighborhood where we once lived. With this understanding, a deep sense of peace began to grow inside me. The pieces of home are coming together, gently guiding me through joyful memories and past challenges.

Insights from the Chapter: Self-Discovery

What I learned from that experience is that self-discovery is a continuous process. Both clarity and confusion shape our journey of understanding ourselves. Sometimes, this leads us to believe things that aren't true. Other times, it makes us so self-conscious that we doubt even those things that are right in front of us.

By embracing our memories, we can accept the fluid nature of our past and recognize the importance of familial love and support. Only by going through the process of self-discovery can we find peace and a renewed understanding of who we truly are.

Two

A New Home, A New Friend

Not long after I turned three, Mama told us we were moving. We were getting a bigger place—a three-bedroom apartment. Our new home wasn't too far from where we had lived before, but far enough that everything felt new. I remember the way Mama said it, her voice steady yet tired as she packed our things into boxes.

"This apartment is too small for all of us now," she said, glancing at all of us—me, my brother, Ray, and my sister, Nette, who were eight and five years older than me. "We need more rooms." I didn't understand much back then, but I liked the idea of having more space. I was the baby girl. I wanted to go with my big sister everywhere, eager to do what she did, though she never wanted me tagging along.

Even though the new apartment wasn't far, it still felt like another world to us. The day after we moved in, Mama let me go outside to play. The apartment buildings were lined up at different angles, with kids running and playing all around them. The sounds of laughter and chatter filled the air. To me, it was a big space, the place where I would spend the next years of my life—where I'd learn to ride a bike, where I'd get all my childhood injuries, and where I'd meet my first real friend.

I remember the day I met my best friend. I was playing in front of our building on the sidewalk, a little unsure of what to do. There were so many kids running around, all older than me, and I wasn't sure if I should join them. Just as I was about to turn back toward the apartment, I saw a girl who looked about my size. She had sandy hair in two pigtails and a smile that lit up her face. She was playing with her toys on the sidewalk.

I walked over, feeling happy and bouncy. She looked up and smiled at me with joy in her eyes.

"Hi! I'm Sharin! What's your name?"

"I'm Faithe!" I said, feeling a bit shy but also really happy. I had never had a friend my age who was a girl before. Back at the apartment where we used to live, the kids were mostly boys. "How old are you?"

"Three!" Sharin said, showing me three fingers. "Today is my birthday!"

I beamed. "Me too! I just turned three last week!"

Sharin's eyes went wide. "We're the same! We can be best friends!"

And just like that, Sharin and I became inseparable. From that day on, Sharin and I enjoyed everything together, keeping nothing from one another. We faced the world side by side. We played every chance we got, running free around the apartment complex as far as our mothers would let us go. Sometimes, we played with our dolls, pretending to cook meals from dirt, grass, and water. We built our little playhouse from old boxes and set it up on the grass, where our imaginations ran wild. On other days, we became daring explorers, crawling through bushes and leaping over sidewalk cracks that we imagined were treacherous ditches ready to swallow us whole if we missed a step.

Our world was just the right size for us. It was a small space between our apartments, the playground, and the sidewalk, but to us, it felt endless. It felt safe as if we could run forever and still be close to home. When the streetlights flickered on, our mothers' voices would echo through the evening air, loud and reassuring, as if they always knew we would come running. But until then, the world was ours to explore.

Sharin and I would skip along as we walked, making up our own silly songs that only we understood. We giggled about everything and nothing, our laughter weaving through the air. We didn't need anyone else; it was just the two of us, side by side as if we had known each other forever.

And in a way, it felt like we had.

Insights from the Chapter: The Gift of Friendship

They say family is the one gift we don't get to choose, given to us by God. But friends? Friends are the family we choose for ourselves—the people we willingly let into our lives, shaping our days and memories. Yet, in my case, I didn't choose my first friend. At the tender age of three, friendship found me in the form of Sharin.

Meeting Sharin was one of the best things that ever happened to me. She was the first person I spoke to after moving to a new home, and though our bond began by chance, it grew into something extraordinary. I didn't choose Sharin, but looking back, I'm deeply grateful that life brought her into my world.

Friends hold a special place in our lives. They are not just companions; they become a part of us. They shape who we are—our personalities, our habits, and sometimes even the course of our lives. Sharin was that kind of friend for me, a constant by my side, teaching me the true meaning of connection and the power of shared laughter and dreams.

Three

Lessons from Shuga

Not only had I found a best friend in Sharin, but there was more to come. As we walked down the sidewalk together, singing and skipping a tradition we created, something else fell into place— an older friend and mentor. Her name was Shuga.

We met her one afternoon. She was in her early twenties, sitting on her porch just as happy as she could be. Her smile shined beyond the ordinary. Her loud laughter drew us in.

“Hey, girls! You two look like trouble—come on over here!” she called, waving us over.

Sharin grinned and whispered excitedly, "Look, she’s funny. We have to go meet her!"

I followed Sharin as we walked up to the porch. “Hi, I’m Faithe,” I said shyly, “This is Sharin.”

“Well, well! Sharin and Faithe. I’m Shuga,” she said with a warm smile. “Y’all know how to cook?”

“A little,” Sharin replied with a mischievous grin.

“I cook with my mama and grandma all the time, but I’d like to learn more,” I said.

Shuga chuckled. "Oh, you're in for a treat then. I'll show you how—just you wait. Ain't nothing like eating the food you made yourself?"

Shuga wasn't like anyone we had ever met before. She was different and in the best possible way. She became our mentor, someone who looked out for us and taught us things we never would've learned on our own. She showed us how to do all kinds of girly things—things that made us feel older, more grown-up. She taught us how to cook breakfast, grits, eggs, and pancakes, which became our weekend ritual. We'd sit at her little table, proudly eating what we'd made ourselves.

But Shuga didn't stop there. She taught us to crochet. Sharin's stitches always looked neater than mine.

"Practice makes perfect, honey," she'd say with a wink, her thick fingers guiding the yarn with a kind of grace you wouldn't expect from someone her size. "Now, honey, with crochet, it's all about practice. See how your stitches come together? Yours is just fine, Faithe. Don't worry about perfection; just keep at it."

Sharin, who always got it right immediately, proudly held up her work. "Mine look neat, don't they?"

Shuga laughed, her voice booming through the room. "Neat and tidy, just like your little self! But watch out—I bet Faithe will catch up in no time."

She also showed us how to play cards—Go Fish, Solitaire, Uno, and her favorite, Spades. Sharin was good at it. I joined in, though I wasn't all that interested. Still, she made it fun, laughing and joking as we played. Sometimes, she'd even let us win just to see the joy spread across our faces.

"Go Fish, y'all!" she would shout with glee. "I know you have that seven. Gimme it!"

"How do you always know?" I would ask, laughing.

"Girl, I've been playing this game since I was knee-high!" Shuga would say with a grin as she dealt the next hand. "But don't think I'll let you win all the time!"

And then there was hair. Shuga could braid like no one else. She showed us how to part our hair perfectly, twist and weave the strands, and add colorful beads that clicked together at the ends. Sharin and I practiced on our dolls, our clumsy fingers fumbling but determined, imitating her every move with wide-eyed focus.

"You think you can braid like this?" Shuga said, demonstrating a perfect twist in the strands of hair. "Come on, try it out."

I struggled to get the braids as tight as Shugas, my hands awkward with the doll's hair. "It's so hard to get them tight!" I complained.

Shuga grinned and gave a nod of encouragement. "You'll get it. Don't rush. One twist at a time."

And dancing—oh, the dancing. Shuga could dance like Rerun on "What's Happening." She loved to sing country songs like "Delta Dawn." We danced around her small living room; her voice was strong and full of heart.

"♫Delta Dawn, what's that flower you have on?" she would sing loudly. "Come on, girls, sing with me!"

We'd giggle as we twirled around her living room. We would even stomp to make the beat of the song.

One day, she kicked Sharin's leg out, making her slip into a Chinese split while I watched in terror.

She said, "Now come on, Faithe, it's your turn!" I got in position, hesitated, and then jumped away when my leg didn't slide all the way down in a split. I imagined something would happen to my legs that would not be good.

"Don't worry. You'll be doin' cheerleader stunts in no time!" Shuga chuckled.

Shuga's size was impossible to ignore—she was obese, but we never thought less of her because of it. If anything, we loved her more for it. She made her own clothes, sewing them together with vibrant fabrics because nothing in the stores would fit her. She was proud of the dresses she wore, even if they were a little too bright or loud for most people's taste. She showed us how she could turn simple fabric into something uniquely her own.

I had noticed the dresses Shuga wore were different colors, unlike any other. Then, one day, I said, "I like your dress, Shuga," noticing the vibrant orange fabric she'd sewn together.

"I made it myself!" Shuga proudly smoothed the fabric down and smiled.

"It's very pretty, and the color stands out," Sharin added.

Shuga replied, "Thank you, baby girl. It's just a simple piece of cloth and a little thread I put together, that makes me feel special since I can't buy the clothes in the stores. That's all that counts."

Shuga had a hard time maintaining good hygiene because she couldn't sit in the tub and take baths. I remember the ambulance having to pry her out of the tub on two occasions after she'd gotten stuck. She held out on calling for help until she had no choice because it embarrassed her.

That made her part of the neighborhood gossip. We overheard someone saying, "How many times does it take for her to call the ambulance to realize she should not try to sit in the bathtub?" Then, with sadness on her face, she said, "Ain't that somethin'?" in an attempt to cover up her emotions.

But neither I nor Sharin cared.

We leaned in and said, "We don't care, Shuga," trying to make her feel less embarrassed.

Then Sharin added, "Yeah, that's not important. You're our friend, Shuga."

Shuga's eyes warmed as she smiled. "I tell ya, you girls are something else!"

She would always welcome us to stay over for girls' night and fun. Sharin's face would light up with excitement. She accepted every time she had the chance once her mother granted permission.

"How about you, Faithe, you sure you don't want to spend the night too?" Shuga asked me once. "Sharin will keep me company. Three would be even better."

"I like being home in my bed at night," I replied, smiling.

Shuga nodded, "I understand, no problem. You can join us whenever you're ready."

We spent many of our days at Shuga's apartment, learning and laughing with her. We were at her house when we weren't outside running around or at each other's houses. In that tiny apartment, we could truly be ourselves. With her, we didn't have to think about anything else—the poverty that surrounded us or the negativity waiting outside in the world. For those moments, it felt like none of it could touch us.

Shuga was an inspiration to us in spite of all her struggles. With her and the numerous lessons she taught us, everything in our small world seemed big. And because of that, we loved and cherished her despite her flaws, problems, and imperfections. We were Shuga's little mentees, and she was our best friend.

Although we were not aware of it at the time, the years we spent with Shuga would shape us in ways we could never have predicted. She taught us much more than just how to cook, dance, or braid hair. She instilled in us the values of acceptance and loving people for who they are rather than what they look like. And that lesson was more important than any ability or knowledge for two little girls growing up in a world that didn't always make sense.

Looking back, I realize now just how much Shuga gave us. She gave us her time, her love, and her wisdom, morals that went far beyond her size. And no matter how far we wandered in life or how much we grew, she remained a part of us just like the stitches in the fabric of our lives, just like those in the dresses she made that fit her perfectly.

Insights from the Chapter: Evolving Through Friendship

Throughout your life, you learn something from every person you meet. Some encounters felt like fleeting moments, while others left a lasting impact. Shuga was one of the people for me—someone who left a lasting impact on my life. She was a mentor who guided, supported, and taught me life skills that shaped not only my abilities but also my character, confidence, and resilience.

Through Shuga, we learned to embrace people for who they are rather than judging them based on appearance or societal standards. Shuga's confidence and self-acceptance taught us how to love ourselves and others despite imperfections.

Together, we learn to find joy in the small moments. Despite the challenges of life, moments of fun, laughter, and connection can provide emotional refuge.

Whether it's cooking, crocheting, or braiding hair, growth comes through practice and patience. After meeting and learning from Shuga, we realized that fun and play are essential components of learning and personal development.

All in all, Shuga taught us the importance of mentorship, kindness, and resilience, as well as the value of embracing differences and finding joy in life's simplest moments.

Four

Shuga's Closet

Childhood was filled with experiences that molded us and made us who we became, even if we didn't understand it at the time. One day, when Sharin and I were about 11 years old, we were at Shuga's apartment. We began playing an innocent game that turned into something much more, a modest but significant moment in understanding identity as we matured.

Sharin and I were hanging out like any other day when a boy named Hershey from the neighborhood stopped around to play. We joked, played cards, and had fun friendship moments. Then suddenly, Shuga, who was always thinking about something exciting, began to mix things up.

She dared Sharin and Hershey to stay in the front room closet with the lights off. It was meant to be a silly game, just something to keep us entertained. But when they stepped inside, Shuga quickly shut the door and locked it. Her real challenge wasn't about staying in the dark—it was about what it would take to get out.

"If you wanna come out, you gotta kiss," she teased.

Sharin sat there, unbothered, as if the whole thing was just another game. But Hershey? He panicked, started to scream, banged on the door, and begged to be let out. He didn't want to take part in it. When Shuga finally opened the door, he shot out like a bullet, looking shaken. Sharin, on the other hand, remained calm and stepped out only when she was ready.

That day, we discovered something we didn't quite grasp yet. The game Shuga played was a moment of self-discovery. Maybe Hershey was terrified to kiss a girl. Perhaps he was scared of what it implied. Or maybe he was simply afraid or uninterested in Sharin. Whatever the case, we didn't judge him. We had heard the whispers in the neighborhood, the rumors about him being "too girly," and maybe this was Shuga's way of testing him. But to us, he was still our friend.

No matter what he preferred, we loved and respected him just the same. In fact, over time, he taught us things about style, confidence, and how to carry ourselves with grace. That day was a lesson—not about him, but about the way we saw each other. In the end, identity isn't something to be tested. It's something we each discover in our own way, in our own time.

Insight from the Chapter: Identity and Acceptance

At that time, the closet incident seemed very insignificant—just another silly game of ours—but deep down, it taught us a very significant lesson about life and about ourselves.

It made us aware of the importance of identity and self-acceptance. For the very first time, we understood that every person has a unique identity and that we should never judge or test them.

Instead, we should embrace, accept, and cherish each other just as we are.

That silly game taught us a precious lesson: nothing is absolutely right or wrong. Everything can be both right and wrong. It all comes down to one simple thing—our perception. The way we see and embrace things makes all the difference.

Five

Moaning Walls

I remember it as if it were yesterday—a warm summer day when the orange and gold bricks of the project buildings glared in the sunlight. My best friend and I, just two little girls, playing in my room. Our little colored dolls were scattered across the floor, their arms flung in every direction. Crayons and coloring books filled the remaining spaces, adding splashes of color on the floor. The scent of charcoal wafted in from outside—my mom was preparing meat for the grill, just as she always did on holidays.

At eight years old, I was full of energy. My hair used to be braided with colorful beads that sparkled and danced with every deliberate shake of my head. My best friend, Sharin, just a few days younger than me, was equally adventurous. She wore her tight, beaded hair, too, though hers was wilder and less tamed. We giggled and played, sharing the kind of laughter that only best friends can create. But as we played, something strange happened—something that cut through our little bubble of innocence like a sharp, cold breeze.

"Did you hear that?" My voice barely murmured, but I remember how my eyes widened and darted to the wall, where there was a chipped layer of paint revealing another color of the wall.

“Hear what?” My best friend replied with a look of mischief in her eyes—always curious, always eager to explore. The light in the room was fading as night was beginning to set in.

I frowned. My eyebrows furrowed in confusion. I leaned my head toward the wall, the spot closest to the noise. “It sounded like... screaming. From next door.”

My best friend was always the outspoken, fun one, quick to speak. Her imagination was ready to make a guess. “Maybe it’s a game! Like hide and seek or something,” she said, with excitement and curiosity in her eyes. I shook my head vigorously while the grin disappeared from my face.

“Nope, it didn’t sound like a game to me. It sounds... strange.”

For a brief moment, Sharin’s brows were wrinkled in thought. Then she jumped up with wonder in her eyes. “Let’s find out!” she said, her voice bursting with determination. I tried to stop her, but she ran to the kitchen, grabbed an empty glass, and ran back into the room, holding it up like a prize.

I bit my lip as the fear in my mind began to show in my eyes, as if something dark and creepy was about to disturb our day. I asked with a shaky voice, “And just how are we going to do that?”

With a smile, Sharin held up the glass as if it were a magical tool. “We use this glass! We can hear better if we put it to the wall and put our ear to it.” Sharin was pressing the glass against the wall with her ear glued to it before I could stop her. I remember hesitating before trying it myself, regardless of the anxiety I felt about what I might hear.

But in the end, my curiosity won, and I finally nodded. The outside world seemed to disappear as we pressed our ears to the glass against the worn-painted wall. There was a brief moment of silence. Then, through the wall came the whispers that became moans heavy in the air. And then, the woman's voice got louder—a straining, desperate, unusual sound to our ears.

"Ooh (murmuring a name we couldn't make out)!" The words cut through the quiet like a knife, sharp and unsettling.

The thought of getting into trouble if my mother came in and found us with the glass to the wall made me flinch with every sound, my heart thumping in my chest. My voice was shaking as I muttered, "It's…it's not a game." I recall my head booming with disbelief as the reality set in.

In contrast, Sharin wrinkled her nose in disgust and pressed her ear closer while her eyes widened. She scrunched her face as if she had just heard something disgusting and said, "Eww." Still picturing Mama entering at any moment, I tried to laugh, but my voice was shaky, and my nerves were still full of fear.

I answered, "Right, eww," but the words didn't bring any relief.

However, Sharin was already recovering, and she was unbent by whatever terrible words we had just heard. Her voice was anxious but still had the innocence of a child who was still trying to make sense of what they had just heard. "We need to go play outside now with these creepy sounds," she sighed.

I nodded, and my courage strengthened. "Yeah, outside," I agreed. We both knew that whatever was happening on the other side of the wall was not for us to understand—not yet. And the thought of playing in the open air, away from the strange sounds that seeped through the walls in Mama's room, was a relief.

With a gentle clatter, we moved away from the wall and put the glass aside. Our faces were filled with a mix of bewilderment and determination. Something far too mature for us to understand disrupted our day of play. However, we were still children, and the summer night outside was waiting for us— to return to the backyard where the sound of laughter could overpower all the other sounds.

I remember how we looked at each other in that instant, our eyes wide and overflowing with unanswered questions. Then, we burst into laughter—laughter that promised to keep our imaginations alive long after the whispering walls had gone silent, laughter that desperately tried to chase away the uneasiness lingering in the air.

We both knew, even if we didn't say it that there were mysteries in the adult world that we weren't ready to confront. And so, we did the only thing we could do— ran outside, away from the whispers, away from the walls.

The rhythm of R&B blues spilled out from the radio, blending with the smoke from the grill and the sounds of our laughter. It all mixed with the events of the neighborhood—music and joy weaving together, a reminder of home amidst the unfolding mystery. As the summer light faded and darkness began to fall, we found satisfaction in the games we played, holding onto a new secret that deepened our friendship and strengthened the bond we shared.

Another world of fantasy awaited us just beyond the door. With one last glance back, we left the echoes of that strange day behind—stepping into a world swirling into the violet and deep blue night.

Insights from the Chapter: Remaining Naive

Remembering the incident now, I realize that children often confront things too big to understand. It offers a vivid and emotional glimpse into the innocence and curiosity of childhood. Curiosity leads children into situations they don't fully comprehend, but their innocence and creativity help them navigate these moments with resilience.

In these moments, we should listen to a child's curiosity when they face the unknown, understanding that not all questions are meant to be answered immediately.

Another lesson I learned that day was that friendship allows us to face fears together. These relationships provide support, comfort, and courage. Even in discomfort, the connection between us helps us process and move forward.

The 'whispering walls' represent the unknown—something beyond the children's understanding that disrupts their innocent world. This teaches us that the world is full of mysteries, some unsettling or beyond our comprehension. It's a reminder that some things are not meant to be understood right away, and it's okay to acknowledge that uncertainty.

Six

The Candy Man on the Hill

Caution had become a way of life for us, though we didn't fully understand why at the time. Sharin and I were always inseparable, like two sides of the same coin. But one day, an encounter changed the way we saw the world around us, forcing us to grow up a little faster than we should have.

Sharin and her mother had moved into a new apartment up on the hill. That hill felt like it divided our world into two different universes, even though it was only a short walk from my house. Sharin and I would spend every free moment together, walking up and down and back and forth between our apartments every day. We passed the same houses, waved to the same neighbors, and followed the same worn path like a well-rehearsed routine.

But there was one house on that hill that we always noticed—the old man's house. Hidden behind a screen porch, it sat back from the road. He was always there, sitting in the shadows, watching. We'd heard whispers about him from other kids—stories that made us uneasy, though we never really talked about it.

One afternoon, as Sharin and I walked up the hill toward her apartment, we heard a raspy voice cut through the stillness of the air.

"Hey, come here for a minute," the voice called out. We looked toward the sound. It was him—the old man. Unseeable, his voice was radiating from his porch, his face hidden behind the screen, but we could make out the glint of his eyes watching us.

"I got some candy," he continued. "Y'all want some?" Sharin and I exchanged disgusted looks as he said, “Come up here and get some candy.” We had heard rumors of terrible people wanting to harm children hidden in the shadows of daily existence—warnings about strangers offering candy. However, at the time, we felt like invincible little souls back then, still too young to think that anything really terrible could happen to us.

We didn't say a word to the old man. Instead, we calmly kept walking down the hill straight to my house. By the time we walked through the front door, gasping for breath, my mother was already up from her chair, her eyes wide with concern.

With a strong voice, she shouted, “What's wrong?” as she saw our horrified faces.

We both shouted it out all at once, our words tumbling over each other in a panic of fear and despair.

“The old man on the hill, Mama! He tried to give us candy! He told us to come to his porch!”

For a moment, my mother's face was unreadable, her lips pressed into a thin line. But then something shifted. Her fury was swift, like a storm gathering on the horizon. She didn't say a word to us. Instead, she grabbed her keys, threw open the front door, and marched up the hill vigorously like Sofia was going to ask Celie why she told Harpo to beat her in the movie “Color Purple.”

We watched from a distance, watching her march with fierce determination. I had never seen her like that before—so full of anger, so ready to confront something dark and hidden. When she reached the old man's house, she didn't hesitate. She stormed up to his porch. We couldn't see beyond the screen or hear what she said, but whatever it was, it struck like a hammer.

From that point on, the old man didn't speak. He didn't offer any more candy and didn't shout back from behind his screen. His arrogant smile went away, and he appeared…frightened for the first time. Whatever Mama said worked. He didn't say another thing to us after that day.

After that, Sharin and I would pass his house every day, but things had changed. He stopped calling out to us from his porch. However, his presence remained in the memories of that day on the hill like a dark stain. We frequently imagined the number of other kids who had heard his voice and received candy from the person behind the screen.

One afternoon, when we passed by, Sharin asked in a low voice that I could barely hear. "How many?"

I said, "I don't know," while avoiding eye contact with the house and instead looking straight ahead.

After that, we never said much about the Candy Man again. We had a mutual agreement we never spoke about that prevented us from probing too far into that dark memory or asking too many questions.

But something had changed. We had lost our sense of security in the world. We were still children and played and laughed as normal, but we were now more cautious since we realized that life wasn't always as simple as it seemed.

We were shielded by my mother's words that day, which were delivered in her rage, which we would never understand. However, after that day, her words were unable to wipe out the awareness that there were people in the world–like the old man on the hill–who could hurt us in ways we weren't yet entirely aware of.

And so, we kept walking up and down that hill, growing a little older, a little wiser, with each step.

Insights from the Chapter: Innocence, Instinct, and Strength

Childhood often involves a sense of invincibility and safety, but some moments force children to face the reality that not everyone has good intentions. In those moments, our sense of security shattered, revealing that the world isn't always as safe or simple as we once believed.

That day, our bond deepened as we silently agreed not to delve further into the dark memory of the 'Candy Man.' Our shared silence revealed how childhood friendships often provide a space to process difficult or unsettling experiences without needing to speak about them.

From that day on, the 'Candy Man' has served as a metaphor for the hidden threats that exist in everyday life—dangers that children may not initially recognize but that adults are aware of. The incident taught us to listen to our instincts, heed the warnings of others, and be mindful of situations that don’t feel right, even when they aren't immediately clear.

This incident provided me with the insight that sometimes a child must decide how to respond to adults who mean them no good when positive adults are not present.

Seven

KTown Hustle Treats and the Blind Lady's Sight Beyond Sight

KTown had its share of struggles, but if there was one thing that made it feel like a true community, it was the food. In every apartment square, someone sold something. It was a village in its own way—one where a child could always find a snack for a few coins. The rental office was the central hub for government-funded boxed lunches in the summertime, filled with bologna sandwiches, chips, a cookie, a piece of fruit, and a carton of milk and orange aid. If you had a quarter, you could head to the back door of a woman from the neighborhood, famous for her cinnamon rolls. Fresh, warm, and tasty with every bite.

Others had their own specialties. There was the woman who sold hotdog sandwiches fried in a skillet, dressed with mustard, ketchup, and pickles, served alongside a bag of chips for just over a dollar. And, of course, the frozen drinks in a paper cup, the cool cup sellers—each apartment square had at least one, but in my square, our ice cream lady's "frosties" were legendary. Unlike the other frozen treats, hers had a secret ingredient that kept them from turning into solid blocks of ice. You could savor the flavor with each slurp or stir it into a smooth, slushy treat.

Then there were the candy stores.

In each square, a makeshift store was run from someone's apartment, selling pickles, bubble gum, chico sticks, and every candy a child could dream of. An old, blind woman owned the one in my square. She had long gray hair and long nails, and her eerie presence made the neighborhood kids whisper that she was a witch. We couldn't fathom how she, being blind, could count her money and keep up with everything so precisely. But somehow, she did.

Her candy was cheap—a penny for a piece, up to fifty cents for something bigger. No matter how poor we were, we could always afford something from her store. That was why what happened that day at the age of 8 years old weighed on me so heavily.

It was supposed to be just another trip for candy. My friends and I walked in, picked up the sweets we wanted, and got ready to pay. Then, one of them slipped me a bag of rock gum from the back and motioned for me to keep it. The others did the same. No words were spoken, but the message was clear: we were about to walk out with more than we paid for.

Fear clawed at my chest, but I did what they did. The blind lady immediately grabbed each kid who had something extra they weren't expecting to pay for, taking it back.

"Where do you think you're going with that? Hand it over," she said, her tone steady but firm.

My friends froze. She turned toward each of them as if she could see. One by one, she grabbed their hands, telling them to put back what they had taken or pay for it. They had been caught.

But she said nothing to me.

My heart pounded. Had she missed me? Did she not know? Or—did she know and choose to let me walk away?

On the outside, I laughed along with my friends once we got away, but on the inside, I felt sick. I couldn't shake the feeling that the blind lady knew. She had caught the others—what made me think I had truly gotten away with it?

That guilt gnawed at me. I couldn't eat the stolen candy. I tried to throw the candy away, but my friends took it and ate it. I couldn't pretend I hadn't done it. A day or so later, I intentionally went to her store to make up for what I had done, afraid she would call me out. But she didn't. She treated me just as she always had. Maybe she really didn't know, or maybe she did, and she was waiting to see what I would do.

I handed her my money and bought some candy—more than I usually would. But I left her extra, more than the cost of what I was buying. When she tried to give it back, I turned and walked away.

I don't know if she ever realized why I did that, but I did. That moment taught me something about myself. It showed me the weight of my choices and the kind of person I wanted to be. I had followed the crowd once, but never again. That day, I learned that integrity wasn't just about getting caught—it was about living with yourself afterward.

Insight from the Chapter: The Weight of a Choice: A Lesson in Integrity

Life has a way of presenting us with defining moments—times when we are presented with a decision that may seem small at the time but has a lasting impact on our souls. That day in the blind lady's store was one of those times for me. It wasn't about the stolen candy or whether I got caught; it was about what I carried with me after.

The truth is, wrongdoing isn't just about who sees or who punishes—it's about you. It's about the voice inside that won't let you rest until you make it right. I didn't face the embarrassment of being caught, but I did face something deeper—my own conscience. The uneasy feeling of knowing I had done something wrong was part of an experience that would shape the choices I made in life.

The blind lady may not have seen me steal, but she saw something beyond sight—perhaps she knew the power of a lesson learned through guilt, through self-reflection, through the decision to make things right on my own. She didn't have to call me out; life did that for me.

Integrity is not about avoiding the consequences; it is about living the right way so you can hold your head high. It is about doing the right thing when no one is watching. That moment in the blind lady candy store was a piece of the mold of who I would become. I learned that life's lessons don't only shape the moment but also the path ahead.

Then, who you become is determined not by what others see or are aware of but by what you know to be true about yourself.

Eight

Finding Faith in KTown

It was our first apartment at 4516 Apt C, 9th Avenue, where my mother, siblings, and I lived, close to my grandmother's apartment. We could walk right out our back door into hers. Our family's life was centered around First Baptist Kingston, which sat right across the street from my grandmother's apartment, just a stone's throw from what was our first apartment in the projects. Grandma was dedicated to her faith. As a member of the usher board, she was always greeting people at the church door on Sunday mornings. Every Sunday, she beamed proudly in her white suit with white gloves, guiding families to their seats. Her grace showed everyone around her the spirit of service. My mother was a proud member of the usher board, too; faith was just as strong. Church was more than a routine for both of them—it was part of who they were.

Sunday School was a weekly ritual in our family. My mother loved that I could recite the books of the Bible aloud before I even turned five. She beamed, watching me proudly as I rattled them off, one after the other. We sang the most inspiring spiritual songs, learned the best faith-based lessons, and had the most comforting routine. First Baptist Kingston was more like a community, not just the church but an anchor that helped shape my young mind and kept my family close to our faith.

When the pastor and his wife eventually moved to a new location, it felt natural for us to follow them. My mother and grandmother wanted to be part of their ministry, supporting them as they had supported us. But after a few years, that feeling began to change. When the new pastor came, we drifted away from that place, no longer finding the same sense of home that we'd had at First Baptist Kingston. My mother started visiting other churches and exploring different congregations. She was dedicated to staying connected to her faith, but nothing ever felt quite like it had in the beginning. I watched her try to make a new church home, but I could tell it was never the same.

When we eventually moved into the larger apartment at 4417B on 9th Terrace North, I was growing up and figuring out my relationship with the church. By then, I didn't have a regular church to attend, but whenever I could, I found myself going back to First Baptist Kingston—especially during Youth Week or when the youth choir was involved. I felt a pull to those familiar pews, the ones where my family had worshiped together so many times. But it was different now; I was older, and the routines that used to feel so close now seemed distant.

By the time we moved to 4417B, I felt the absence of our close-knit church family. I remember Mama was still searching for the right fit, attending different services here and there, but nothing ever quite stuck. I guess it was the same for me as a child. I remember attending a little Methodist church just across from our apartment for vacation Bible school every summer. One summer, my best friend encouraged me to join. She had been going on her own and always returned with stories and crafts to share. Her enthusiasm was contagious. I hesitated, like the shy girl I was. I didn't talk much and wasn't sure how to blend in sociably. Yet, she encouraged me to join her.

Vacation Bible school was a joy. I can still taste the cookies and juice we had for snacks, small comforts that somehow made the time there feel safe and welcoming. My best friend and I would sit together, sometimes quietly and sometimes whispering when we thought no one could hear us. We learned Bible stories and sang songs. Each day, we crafted small treasures to take home. I loved showing Mama what I had made. Those days at the little Methodist church felt like a bridge to continue the faith I'd known. It wasn't the same as First Baptist Kingston, but it was a place to grow and learn, to feel grounded.

The church, in whatever form it took, was always there, shaping who I was. Whether it was in Sunday School at First Baptist Kingston, following Mama to different churches, or making crafts at vacation Bible school, the lessons of faith and community were always with me. I learned the value of kindness from watching my grandmother welcome everyone with a warm smile, I learned the strength of commitment from my mother's search for a church home, and I learned that even if things changed, there was always something to help keep us grounded.

Church was more than just a place to go on Sundays; it was a connection to my family, a sense of belonging, and a source of strength that has remained with me, even as the years and addresses changed.

Insights from the Chapter: Family Influence, Spiritual Growth, and Faith

Faith and community are foundational in shaping one's identity and belief system. Religious communities, far beyond just places of worship, serve as pillars of belonging, support, and connection. Through my own experience, I learned how a close-knit community can provide a sense of stability and strength during times of transition and uncertainty.

My mother and grandmother embodied resilience, dedication, and kindness, becoming powerful role models for how family can profoundly influence one's personal growth and spiritual life. The lesson here is clear: family offers guidance, emotional support, and comfort, especially when navigating life's challenges.

Our experience of moving away from a church that once felt like home teaches a valuable lesson about the inevitability of change. Whether it's a shift in place, community, or routine, the core values and lessons we carry from those experiences remain with us. The key takeaway is the importance of embracing change while holding steadfast to the values that matter most.

Even the smallest childhood moments—like attending Vacation Bible School or singing in church—can leave lasting impressions. These formative years play a critical role in shaping one's character, spiritual journey, and understanding of community. Seemingly minor experiences often lay the foundation for a lifelong path.

Despite changes in church environments, my family's unwavering commitment to faith remained a guiding force. This illustrates that while external circumstances may evolve, it is crucial to hold on to core values like kindness, service, and spiritual growth.

Through the examples set by my mother and grandmother, I learned the profound impact of service to others. Acts of kindness—whether through welcoming someone into a church or supporting loved ones—leave a lasting legacy and can bring a deep sense of fulfillment.

This time of my childhood taught me the enduring power of faith, the importance of family, and the strength to adapt to life's changes while staying true to the values that define us. These lessons continue to resonate, shaping who I am today.

Nine

The Spirits of KTown

Back in KTown, I always felt something creepy about that two-story, three-bedroom apartment. Strange things began to happen right after we moved in, phenomena that my mother sensed but could not completely describe. The apartment seemed to have a life of its own, a haunting spirit that breathed eerie energy into the walls, floors, and furniture and crept into our dreams. When we kids were old enough to sense it, we didn't talk about it, but we all knew something was off.

My brother and sister shared a room in our smaller, two-bedroom apartment before we moved into the three-bedroom one. I slept with Mama. The photos I had seen of my sister and brother in the same room, sleeping in twin beds, provided the evidence since I was too young to remember that time. But when we moved to the bigger apartment, things changed. My sister and I shared a room with twin beds while my brother finally got a room of his own. Despite that, I was still Mama's baby, always ending up in her bed no matter where I fell asleep. I used to think it was some kind of magic like I'd dream of being in my bed but would wake up in Mama's room. Later, I learned that it was Mama who moved me, carrying me in her arms after I had fallen asleep.

Before long, the oddities started. All of us began to have nightmares and dark, strange dreams that persisted long after we awoke. I vividly recall one night when my sister woke me up. Though her voice sounded low, as if she wasn't awake, what she said next had me creeped out and baffled.

"Look at that snake coming into the room!" She pointed to the ceiling above the door with her eyes wide open yet unfocused, as if caught between sleep and consciousness, she demanded while sitting upright in her bed.

"What?" I said while rubbing my eyes, trying to get rid of my sleepiness.

"That snake," she repeated. "It's a piece of wire. It's coming into the room."

She lay back down like nothing had happened, and within seconds, she was asleep again, her breathing steady and deep. I lay there frozen, staring at the spot where she had pointed, but I saw nothing—just shadows moving across the door, cast by the dim light filtering in from the hallway. Still, I couldn't shake the feeling that something was watching us.

It wasn't just my sister. My brother had his own terrifying experiences in that apartment. When he was about 15 or 16, he had a dream that shook the entire house. I'll never forget that night. Mama and I were asleep in her room when, suddenly, we were jolted awake by my brother's scream. A scream so loud, so full of terror that my heart stopped for a second. Then we heard the slam of his bedroom door.

He came barreling into Mama's room, diving onto the bed, his face pale and his body trembling. Mama sat up, her voice sharp with fear.

"What in the world is wrong with you?"

His words tumbled out, panicked and fast. "The Grim Reaper was trying to take me! He was standing over me, and then—he pulled the covers over my head!"

Mama just held him but didn't say much after. She whispered prayers as we all sat huddled on the bed, the darkness in the room feeling heavier than usual. After that night, my brother never really talked about it again, but the look in his eyes was enough to tell us that he'd never forget.

Years later, when my brother left for the Air Force, I inherited his room. I thought I'd be fine. I had grown older, maybe a little braver, too, but the apartment had a way of reminding you that it held the upper hand. One night, I experienced something that made my skin crawl. I didn't see the Grim Reaper, but the bed—the head of my bed—began to sink slowly, as if something invisible was pressing down on it. The weight grew heavier, pulling me into the mattress. My heart pounded, but instead of screaming, I began to pray. I recited the Lord's Prayer, then the 23rd Psalm. As I whispered the words, the bed slowly started to rise again, the pressure easing until everything was back to normal. I lay there, clutching my blanket, too afraid to sleep but too scared to move.

Mama always had a deep fear of that apartment. She was sensitive to things that the rest of us couldn't quite grasp. There were nights when she would hear things—voices, whispers calling her names, taunting her. I remember sitting on the side of her bed one evening. She was crying softly, her hands shaking.

"What's wrong, Mama?" I asked, as I remained calm. My empathy grew just from feeling her anxiety and seeing her in that state of being.

With a voice hardly audible above a whisper, she said, "I hear voices." "They keep saying horrible things to me and calling me bad names."

I grabbed her hand and held it. "Mama, don't listen to them. You're a good mama, a good person. Don't let them get to you."

She nodded, but I could tell it was hard for her. The apartment had a way of breaking you down, of making you question things you'd never doubted before.

Then, there was that eerie old woman who lived next door. She made sure things didn't get any easier for us. She was strange from the start. She was always watching us when we were in her sight. She would always bang on the walls to let us know that she was there, listening, watching, and waiting. My friends and I would play with our little Fisher Price dolls on the front porch, their small plastic bodies only a few inches high. But those dolls didn't stay with me for long. Somehow, they would go missing. One by one, they'd vanish without a trace.

I once looked over at the old woman's window as I was sitting on the porch. Fisher Price dolls were neatly lined up on the windowsill like the rank of an Army lined up for war. Fisher Price dolls that were exactly the same as mine. My gut wrenched as I got sick to my stomach. Were those mine? Did she take them? We never confronted her about it or said anything. However, I couldn't get rid of the accusations that were circulating about her—that she practiced voodoo and that she performed weird rituals to manipulate or bring harm to people. I couldn't help but worry whether my dolls in her window were a part of something wicked.

There was always the presence of KTown's ghost. We knew we weren't alone in that hot brick apartment, whether it was the elderly woman and her dolls or the weird dreams that kept us restless and broke us from our sleep at night. Something always felt heavy in the air, something that watched, waited, and occasionally alerted us to its presence.

KTown wasn't just a simple location. Despite our best efforts to ignore it, it was alive and full of mysteries and ghosts that would never let us forget.

Insights from the Chapter: Overcoming Individual Fear

The experiences we encountered in KTown made me realize just how deeply a space can influence one's emotional and mental state. The eerie atmosphere of our apartment—filled with strange phenomena, nightmares, and supernatural occurrences—demonstrated how a person's environment can foster lasting fear, anxiety, and uncertainty, ultimately impacting relationships and personal growth.

Although we all experienced unsettling events, we rarely spoke about them openly. Our hesitation to communicate these fears only heightened the tension. Over time, I came to understand that discussing our fears and strange experiences could alleviate emotional burdens and prevent anxiety from escalating, promoting shared understanding and healing.

Despite the fear and bizarre happenings, the unwavering support of my family became a source of strength. Mama's protective instincts and the way we siblings comforted each other made me deeply appreciate the power of family. In the face of difficulty—even the supernatural—our bond was a pillar of resilience.

Living in that apartment also taught me how belief in the supernatural and the unseen can shape one's worldview. The unsettling events challenged our understanding of reality, revealing how unexplained forces can significantly influence our lives. It became clear that the line between reality and the supernatural can often blur.

In essence, this period of my life imparted invaluable lessons on the psychological weight of fear, the strength of family bonds, the complexities of unresolved trauma, and the necessity of confronting and understanding the unknown.

Ten

Sunday's Best and Grandma's Table

Grandma, with her immaculate white usher coat and spotless gloves, used to stand at the doorway of First Baptist Kingston every Sunday. Greeting everyone was her responsibility as the usher, and she did it uniquely. With a firm, no-nonsense tone, she'd smile and offer her greetings to the congregation, reminding anyone with gum to "spit that out before the Lord's house, honey." Her warmth was legendary, but she also kept everyone in line, embodying that rare blend of tough and sweet that only Grandma could pull off.

I remember seeing Grandma stand at her post by the door of First Baptist Kingston in her pristine white suit, white gloves, and the kind of no-nonsense expression that shows both authority and warmth. She nods and smiles at the steady stream of churchgoers, a mix of young and old.

My Grandma always had a way of mixing authority with just the right touch of affection. She used to show authority to the youngsters in a certain sweet way. I remember one time she said to a teenager chewing gum as he walked in the church doors. "Good morning, young man! Wait a minute." She pointed to his mouth. "What are you carrying there? You are aware that gum is not allowed in God's house. Now, honey, throw that in the garbage for me." He obeys politely. She then smiled and softened her tone. "Thank you, baby. Go ahead and have a seat now. Also, don’t let me catch you slouchin’ in that seat!"

Another memory that stood out to me was when I saw Grandma assist an elderly woman. Grandma gave a warm smile and reached out to gently take the hand of that woman who appeared a little tired and worn down as she entered: “Good morning, Sister! You just walk right in now. Allow the Lord to grant you rest today by taking a seat where you choose.” Her voice softened as she paused. “And don't you worry about a thing–you’re exactly where you need to be.”

Grandma’s influence extended even outside the church. She was the unofficial baker for First Baptist Kingston, and everyone knew it. In the week leading up to Sunday, she’d be busy filling orders for the folks who’d put in requests the week before. She was the go-to for cakes, pies, cookies, and her famous homemade peach cobbler that people were willing to wait an extra week for. After church, there’d be a line at her house, people picking up their Sunday orders or putting in a fresh one for the next week.

Being raised on a farm, Grandma kept her recipes and methods simple, traditional, and heartfelt. Everything from scratch—no shortcuts. She’d learned it all growing up in the countryside, where she picked fruit herself and measured sugar by taste and feel rather than cups and spoons. Her house was always filled with the smell of something baking, the aroma trailing out the door, inviting everyone to stop by.

On those Sundays, after ushering the congregation to their seats and keeping everyone in check, she'd head home to her own Sunday dinner, a table filled with country-style cooking and freshly baked desserts.

"Alright, get your orders in early; I'm making peach cobbler this week," she'd announce after service, her face beaming with pride.

"She's got her hands in everything, doesn't she?" one of the ladies would say, watching Grandma's post-church baking tradition in full swing.

"Better be glad she does!" another would reply with a grin, already plotting her next order of sweet potato pie.

For Grandma, baking wasn't just a pastime. It was her way of staying connected with her community and with her faith. Just as she had served in the church, she served the neighborhood with every bite. People came to rely on her for that familiar taste, for the assurance that someone was taking care of them with flour, sugar, and a little bit of love.

Insights from the Chapter: Inheriting Love, Faith, and Service

Grandma's unique blend of authority and warmth taught me that kindness and firmness can coexist. Grandma showed how love and discipline could work together to uplift and guide others. Another thing that I learned from my Grandma was that serving others, even in small ways, can leave a lasting impact on their lives.

Grandma's faith wasn't confined to church only—it was evident in how she greeted every person at the church door and in the care she poured into her baking. Through her example, I understand that faith is best expressed through everyday acts of service, kindness, and love.

The most significant thing Grandma taught me is that a kind word, a gentle smile, or a helping hand can make all the difference to someone in need.

Eleven

The Comfort of Family

Our first apartment was located just behind Grandma's. It often made me feel like we were part of an extended, close-knit family village. Mama handled everything she needed to because we were only a few steps away from Grandma's house. Grandma was always there—welcomed us with open arms and laughter that seemed to echo through the neighborhood. She loved kids and had a knack for making anyone feel at home, which meant that her house was often filled not only with us but with other neighborhood kids, too.

Grandma was very nurturing. Her home was a safe and comfortable place for all of us. The moment we smelled the aroma of her food rising through the air, we rushed to get a taste and be fed. Fresh out of the oven desserts—the fragrance of her delicious biscuits would entice us like a magnet. Her kitchen was a cozy little space. We would stand on counter stools and chairs while she taught us some of her cooking secrets over bubbling pots.

It was a rite in and of itself to cook with Grandma. She would give us assignments as though imparting valuable family knowledge, such as how to knead bread or make the ideal biscuit dough properly. We excitedly observed her while she skillfully seasoned vegetables or mixed cake batter, taking in every motion she made.

Grandma would say something like, "Now, don't overdo the flour." with a soft, patient tone of voice. She would tell us, "The dough should have a pillow-like texture."

We learned our way around the kitchen, stirring, chopping, and tasting under her guidance. We were so proud when we made a dish that Grandma declared was "just right." Her love for cooking was passed on to us through her patience and love for us. Her kitchen is where we learned that food was more than just something to eat. It was a way of showing care, bringing people together, and passing down a legacy.

Even when we weren't helping in the kitchen and playing outside, Grandma's laughter would still blend with the noises of our happiness as she watched us from behind the door or the porch. She occasionally called us to the porch for a break and served us a feast of fresh watermelon cut into wedges so we could enjoy every bite. I remember the sweet juice pouring down my chin. It was a simple summertime joy.

We also spent time with her cleaning vegetables, laughing and telling stories while shocking peas and snapping green beans out on the porch on summer days. Every task felt so important, like a little piece of a bigger family tradition. Grandma taught us not just how to cook but also how to appreciate the ingredients, the colors, the textures, and the flavors of the seasons.

We learned a lot of traditions from Grandma, from preparing food to gathering around the table for meals that felt like celebrations, even on the simplest of days.

Her role extended beyond her own grandkids; she was the community's grandmother. If other kids were over, in no time, Grandma had them peeling potatoes, snapping beans, or learning to mix up a batch of cornbread. She treated each of us like family, nurturing us in a way that made her house feel like the heart of the neighborhood.

Mama knew she could count on Grandma when she needed a break from the kids, assistance, or just a moment to rest. We could go to her house and be accepted without hesitation. Everyone was taken care of and had a place in Grandma's world. We didn't just learn how to cook and bake from her; we knew what it meant to belong, to love, and to create a nurturing home.

The neighborhood was filled with families just like ours, a network of aunts, uncles, and cousins who all looked out for each other. But Grandma's house was the place everyone knew they could turn to. Her home was a sanctuary, her kitchen a gathering place, and her love a constant reminder that family, no matter how close or distant, was the center of everything.

Insights from the Chapter: Molded by Tradition

Grandma's house was more than a residence to me—it was a sanctuary filled with love, warmth, and acceptance. Her place taught me that creating a home isn't just about physical space but about fostering a sense of belonging and safety for everyone who enters.

Cooking with Grandma wasn't just about making food; it was about preserving family traditions and connecting through shared experiences. She passed down skills, knowledge, and love through simple yet meaningful activities like cooking and storytelling.

In Grandma's home, I came to understand how one person's kindness and openness could bring people together, turning a single house into the heart of a community. She taught us how to find beauty and happiness in life's simplest moments. These small rituals became cherished memories, showing that love and connection are often found in everyday acts.

In Grandma's world, I found not only lessons in cooking but also deeper truths about love, belonging, and the enduring power of family traditions. These lessons became a foundation for understanding the value of connection and the role of community in shaping a meaningful life.

Twelve

KTown Elementary

At Kingston Elementary, we grew up together, learning about friendship, life, and even ourselves along the way. The building itself wasn't particularly impressive – just a simple boxy structure with groaning doors that we could always count on to creak when we pushed them open and paint that was flaking here and there. But inside those familiar walls, the stories of children like me, all going through that crazy yet wonderful stage of life, filled the air.

One of the first things everyone remembers about KTown Elementary is the food. Now, I know cafeteria food doesn't usually get the best reputation, but ours? It was something else entirely. We had the best breakfasts and lunches, the kind that had us looking forward to the cafeteria line every day. There were these small square pizzas with crumbly cheese on top, sometimes paired with crispy French fries. And on those special days when the lunch lady cooked up homestyle meals, we'd get a plate of meatloaf with mashed potatoes and a heap of corn. But the star of the show was always dessert: cinnamon rolls.

Our lunchroom cook was a local legend. She didn't just make cinnamon rolls for the school; she made them for the whole neighborhood, selling them from the back door of her apartment in the projects for 50 cents apiece. It was a sweet deal—literally—and her cinnamon rolls were the stuff of legend. They were perfectly soft and sticky, and the slight smelled just enough like cinnamon to make you forget any problem for a moment.

Once we finished our lunches, we would head straight out to the playground. With monkey bars, slides, and an almost endless running area, it was massive to us as kids. One of my favorite pastimes was flipping across the playground. I remember my fourth-grade year – I must've looked like a little gymnast, doing flip after flip, counting each one like it was an accomplishment. I got a little too ambitious. I kept flipping until I was dizzy and out of breath, my head spinning as I stumbled around.

"You okay?" my teacher called out, with concern in her eyes. "Go inside and get some water. Cool off a bit."

I did as she said, but I was so dizzy I could barely walk straight. I headed toward the playground's exit, trying to keep my balance. Before I knew it, I was face-to-face with one of those old, rusty metal poles by the fence gate. I didn't even have time to brace myself. I smacked into it – hard. When I came to my senses, I tasted blood and felt something sharp. I'd broken one of my front teeth clean in half.

The next week, I came to school with a yellow-tinted, temporary filling. I was grateful to have it, but kids are kids, and that yellow tooth made me the punchline of every joke for the next few years until my mother could afford to fix it in my eighth-grade year going to high school. I'd cover my mouth every time I laughed, a habit that stuck with me even after the tooth was fixed. I guess that yellow tooth became part of my "shy" persona at KTown Elementary, even though shyness wasn't really my thing.

At Kingston Elementary, fights after school were as regular as the afternoon bell that rang to end each school day. That bell was more like a signal for a fight. Every afternoon, a crowd would gather outside to see who was throwing fists that day. Some kids rushed to be in the thick of it, while others dashed to get home and avoid being dragged in. I was lucky. I never ended up in a fight, and I think that was partly because I was likable enough that no one wanted to mess with me. In fact, the real fighters—the ones who knew how to throw down—would look out for me.

"Nah, leave her alone," one of them would say if someone tried to pick on me. "She's cool. She doesn't deserve any of this."

Now, don't get me wrong; I could fight if I had to. Growing up with my older sister, Net, who liked to test my patience, taught me a few moves on the many occasions we tangled in that apartment when Mama was gone or at work. But at Kingston Elementary, I was a quiet kid who kept to myself, did my own thing, and avoided any trouble because I didn't start any.

Kingston Elementary was where we started discovering ourselves and who we were. We were all kids, of course, but we became more aware of our own identities, our likes, and our dislikes. I remember there was a girl in my 6th-grade class who liked me, but I didn't feel the same way. I didn't like girls that way. Still, we got along well, and she accepted that without question. It was simple back then. We knew who we were, and we didn't feel any need to hide it or to push anyone to be something they weren't. Respecting each other's individuality was just part of life.

Uniqueness was taken seriously at Kingston Elementary and in our community. Being different from one another felt like a challenge we all embraced. It was accepted that you should switch things up and find something that would set you apart from the others. If you spotted someone wearing the same outfit or rocking the same hairstyle as you, then it was time to change it up. That was a way to stand out from what other people were doing, whether it was in their clothing style or something as simple as their hairstyle. We all wanted to be unique. We all valued that spirit of creativity and used it to find our own identities.

In retrospect, I see that KTown Elementary was more than just a school. It was a place that molded us and taught us how to navigate the world, the people in it, and ourselves and ourselves – in addition to our ABCs.

Insights from the Chapter: Elementary Lessons of Resilience, Belonging, and Camaraderie

Kingston Elementary, or "KTown" as we called it, was more than just a school—it was a community, a proving ground, and a place where we all began shaping who we were. The school itself wasn't fancy, but its worn-down walls held stories of friendships, growing pains, and life lessons that stuck with us long after we left.

Food was at the heart of our memories, especially those legendary cinnamon rolls. The lunchroom cook wasn't just feeding us; she was a neighborhood icon, selling her sweet, sticky treats to anyone lucky enough to get their hands on one. Lunchtime wasn't just about eating—it was about comfort, connection, and looking forward to something special each day.

Recess brought its own adventures, from playground acrobatics to hard-learned lessons—like the time I flipped one too many times and walked straight into a metal pole, breaking my front tooth. That yellow-tinted temporary filling became part of my identity, teaching me resilience and self-consciousness in equal measure.

Fights after school were part of the rhythm of life, but I was lucky to have people looking out for me. KTown taught us about loyalty, individuality, and respect. It wasn't just a school—it was the first place we truly belonged.

Thirteen

KTown Battles and Bonds

Growing up in KTown was an early lesson of what kind of friends you had. A fight didn't end a bond. It tested it. And if it could survive that, it could survive almost anything.

There was a time when my own friendship was pushed to that edge. Sharin and I were about Ten, sitting on the curb on the side of Shuga's apartment, playing with our dolls and minding our business. We had our dolls in our laps, happily lost in our own little world. Sharin was my girl, my play partner, my solid friend. We weren't doing much but having fun. Then along came Aan, a bigger girl known for starting stuff. Aan was a fighter. Not just someone who could fight but someone who loved to fight. She looked at us, then looked at me and said, "I bet you can't beat her."

That was all it took. In KTown, a challenge like that was not to be ignored. Aan had been pressured by older kids in the same way that she was now daring me to face. Even though I didn't want to, I felt the pressure. Aan knew she couldn't fight us herself, not without looking like a bully, so she did the next thing. She made me fight my friend. And that day, I let myself be pushed.

The fight didn't last long. Sharin ended up falling, hitting her bottom lip on the curb. She had to get stitches. I felt awful, and I still do when I think about it.

What happened that day wasn't just kids being kids. It was pressure, manipulated like play. Aan wasn't testing my strength; she wanted to see how much control she could have over us. I gave in, but Sharin taught me grace and what it means to forgive without hesitation. That kind of friendship is rare. The only fight Sharin and I ever had was manipulated by someone else.

Insights from the Chapter: Lessons In Loyalty, Forgiveness, and Growing Up Tough

What happened between me and Sharin wasn't unusual in KTown. Fights were a traditional part of growing up. As kids, we disagreed, brawled, and dared each other, which was a test that only proved our loyalty. It sounds strange, but most of the time, those fights didn't tear friendships apart. They made them stronger.

We learned early how to read people, how to stand our ground, and how to make peace without ever saying the words. Forgiveness wasn't always spoken aloud. It was shown in how you passed the ball the next day, how you shared your candy or things you cherished the most. That was KTown: unspoken, unwritten, but understood.

The older kids looked out for the younger ones, even while giving us a hard time. We passed down games, dares, and stories. And even though we didn't have much, we had each other to bond with beyond the heat, the concrete bricks, and tough lessons.

Everything in KTown had meaning, even the smallest things. A look could settle an argument. A handshake could seal a pact. And a fight could mark the beginning of a lifelong friendship if you knew how to come back from it. That was the tradition: not just surviving the moment but showing up again the next day like nothing had changed because, deep down, everything had. That kind of loyalty was everything in KTown.

Fourteen

A Journey Toward Forgiveness

It's hard to forgive, but it's a powerful thing. When I was a teenager, a single incident destroyed my family's stability and caused me to carry anger, fear, and pain for many years. The light in my life, my brother Ray, left home for military life as a smart, tall, and healthy young man with the best sense of humor. His experiences in the military changed him in ways we never expected. I had always looked up to him—he had joined the Air Force at just 17, still in high school, after participating in the ROTC, which instilled in him the discipline of military life. He left home a modest, innocent teenager, but when he returned home after his service, he wasn't the same. The experience had given him structure, but it had also introduced him to things that would lead him down a darker path—alcohol, smoking, and drugs.

We lived in the projects, a place where drugs were as common as the everyday struggle. My brother, with his newfound knowledge, shared what he had learned about preparing and using drugs with the neighborhood boys. He had become someone different—someone we didn't fully understand. Inside our apartment, my mother, sister, and I had no idea what he was doing when he stepped outside. We still saw him as the brother we had grown up with, unaware that the streets were claiming him in ways that would soon terrify us.

I'll never forget that day. I was in the kitchen cooking when Angelo, one of the boys my brother hung out with, came knocking at our back door. The wooden door was open, and only the screen door stood between us. When I went to see who it was, my heart stopped—I found myself staring down the barrel of a rifle. Angelo was holding it, his eyes full of anger. "Where's your brother? He's got my $10," he said, his voice low but filled with fury.

My mind raced. I didn't know how to respond; I didn't even process the gravity of the situation. He didn't move, just stared at me through the screen, gun still pointed in my direction. I backed away, shouting, "Boy, what is wrong with you? Stop playing!" But it wasn't a game. I ran to find my sister, who was outside. When I told her what happened, she looked shocked.

"He pointed the rifle at me, too!" she exclaimed.

Without wasting a moment, she ran inside, yelling at our brother in her outspoken way. "Whatever you did, you better go handle it! He pointed a rifle at us!" My brother looked up, calm but focused. "What?"

"He pointed a rifle at us! He's talking about how you owe him $10!"

We called the police, but by the time they arrived, the rifle was gone—a neighbor had hidden it so Angelo wouldn't get into trouble. The police advised him to leave the neighborhood since his family no longer lived there, but the threat didn't go away.

Later, I overheard my uncle speak quietly to my brother. "If you ever pull a gun on someone, you better be ready to use it," he warned. "Because if you don't, they'll come back and kill you." My brother looked up to my uncle and soaked in that advice.

Those words haunted me, knowing how protective my brother was over our household. He was the only male there with us, and three females: my mother, sister, and myself. I had no idea how soon those words would take on an even darker meaning.

It wasn't long after that we heard the gunshots—six of them.

My heart sank, and a cold fear settled over me as someone came running to tell us that my brother had shot Angelo. The people who saw the incident said Angelo had retrieved his rifle back from the neighbor and had kept it in his pickup truck. My brother had gone to confront him about threatening us with the rifle and the money issue. As Angelo turned to run for his truck, my brother shot him – and ended his life.

My brother walked away, straight to my uncle's house, before eventually surrendering himself to the police.

When the trial came, my brother was released. It was ruled self-defense, but that didn't bring peace. Angelo's family was devastated. His brother made a terrifying threat—to kill me, the youngest sister, as revenge for my brother killing his younger brother. I lived in constant fear for months, never knowing if my existence was safe in the only home I had ever known.

The trial wasn't the end of the hell we were going through. My brother ended up in jail after getting into additional trouble, and every time he was up for parole, his murdered friend's parents were present and testified against his release. They couldn't let go of the pain of losing their son, and I couldn't blame them. My brother was imprisoned for 16 years, and the burden of what had transpired seemed to increase with every year that went by. From the beginning of his incarceration, my mother's mental state began to change from the heartbreak of losing her son to prison. It seemed like an unbreakable curse.

Then, yet something happened that I never would have thought was possible.

Angelo's parents stood up at one of my brother's parole hearings. I remember holding my breath, expecting that they would make another appeal to the board to keep my brother incarcerated. Instead, they walked up to the podium and said, "By the grace of God, we have forgiven him. Let him go so he can spend time with his family."

Forgiveness. After all those years, all that pain, they had found a way to forgive my brother. It was a moment that felt like a miracle, a release of the chains that had bound us all. My sister and I, who had been there at the hearing, walked outside to find the boy's parents, our hearts still racing. My sister and I approached the parents slowly, thankfully but not knowing what to say. My sister stepped forward first.

“Thank you,” she whispered, her voice trembling. “Thank you for your forgiveness.”

The boy’s mother smiled, her eyes filled with sorrow but also peace. “It was the grace of God,” she said. “We had to let go to find our own peace.”

I couldn’t hold back the tears any longer. I stepped forward and hugged her, the mother of the boy my brother had killed, and she held me as though we had both been waiting for this moment for years.

My sister said with strong emotion, “We’ve been praying for you and your family,”

I added, “We always pray for your family’s peace.”

“And we’ll pray for yours,” the boy’s father replied. “Enjoy time with your brother. We’ve carried this for so long, but it’s time to let it go.”

Since then, I have prayed constantly for their family’s safety, inner peace, and the strength to continue living without their son. I will never take their forgiveness for granted because I know it cost them much.

After a few years, the incident got me thinking about how to forgive people. One day, I sat down with my now older brother to talk about a question I had been putting off for years.

“Are you upset that you were imprisoned for 16 years longer than necessary?” I asked.

His demeanor was attentive as he gazed at me. "No," he muttered. "It was necessary. Those years were the result of the decisions I made. I learned a lot more about life and myself throughout that period of having to deal with the repercussions of my actions."

I could see the weight he bore and the wisdom engraved in his features, as well as the peace and calm spirit he had discovered within it. He went on, "Forgiveness is for ourselves, not just for those who forgive us." "I had to forgive, too. It's part of healing."

At that moment, I realized that forgiveness isn't linear. It's a journey we all must take, and sometimes that journey twists and turns. But through those twists, we find light and the possibility of moving forward together.

I understand that forgiveness is not about forgetting; it's about freeing yourself from the chains of bitterness and anger. It's about finding peace.

Forgiveness didn't just free my brother. It freed us all.

Insights from the Chapter: The Power of Forgiveness, Healing, and Redemption

Forgiveness is rarely easy, but it is one of the most powerful forces in life. This chapter explores a deeply personal journey through pain, fear, and, ultimately, healing. It begins with my tight-knit family torn apart by the unexpected consequences of my brother's return from military life. Once a beacon of humor and strength, Ray came home changed, introducing habits that led him down a dangerous path—one that entangled the entire family in a world of violence and uncertainty.

The moment that shattered my sense of security was a rifle pointed at me, all over a $10 debt. What started as a threat quickly escalated into tragedy. Ray, in a moment of confrontation, took another young man's life, setting off a chain of fear, retaliation, and years of imprisonment. The weight of that decision hung over my family, with the victim's family refusing to let go of their grief and anger—understandably so.

But then, something unexpected happened. The boy's parents, who had once fought against Ray's parole, stood up in court and forgave him. Their words, "Let him go so he can spend time with his family," changed everything. That moment was a lesson in grace—proof that forgiveness is not about forgetting but about releasing pain to find peace. Ultimately, forgiveness did not just free Ray. It freed us all.

Fifteen

Fun Times in KTown

Life in KTown wasn't just about spooky tales or eerie moments—there were times that felt like pure freedom when the whole neighborhood came alive with joy. I remember the nights when we kids were allowed to stay out late, long after the streetlights came on and the air buzzed with excitement. The best nights were the ones when our mothers were outside listening to music and socializing; no one called us in to come in the house early, and we could run wild like we owned the night.

The playground was the heart of our adventures. Every group of apartments had one in the center, and that's where we'd gather for games of baseball. The bases were anything we could find, and we'd use any small ball. I'll never forget someone standing at the plate, bat in hand, while someone pitched the ball. They hit the ball that echoed through the air, then swung the bat away, and the game was on. "Run!" they'd scream, and we'd sprint around the bases, heart pounding, laughter all around.

When we weren't on the playground, we were tearing through the streets on bikes, skateboards, or roller skates, doing tricks and stunts up and down the hills or racing each other on the pavement. But my favorite activity—one that my best friend and I loved more than anything—was jumping. We jumped off anything and everything. The metal sliding board in the playground. We'd climb to the top of the back stairway, look down, and leap off like we were invincible. It never crossed our minds to be afraid; the thrill of the jump was all that mattered.

At home, we didn't stop jumping either. Our apartment building had thirteen concrete stairs, and jumping from the very top to the bottom was a challenge we couldn't resist. "Bet you can't make it this time!" one of us would tease. With a determined grin, we'd take a deep breath and jump—legs stretched out, arms flailing for balance, hearts racing as we soared through the air and landed with a thud. Somehow, we never got hurt, but each time felt like we were flying.

Then, there were the sticker bushes in front of our porches. These large, prickly bushes sat there, daring us to jump over them. And we did—again and again, testing how far we could leap without getting pricked by the sharp thorns. It was risky, but that made it more exciting. We'd race up to the bushes, launch ourselves over them, and land on the other side feeling proud of our fearlessness.

On calmer days, we'd pick fruit from the trees scattered around the neighborhood—figs, peaches, apples, and pecans. We'd fill our pockets with the ripest ones, sneaking in the people who own houses and yards, climbing the trees to get the best fruit. We were like scavengers on a treasure hunt.

Summer days were filled with dodgeball, played against the brick walls of the apartment buildings. The ball would smack against the wall with a loud thud, and we'd scramble to dodge it. If we weren't dodging balls, we were playing hide and seek or our neighborhood's special twist—"Hide and Go Get." The game, where the boys chased the girls, was always met with shrieks of laughter as we darted between buildings, breathless and giggling. One time, I looked back to see how far the boy was, and when I turned to look back in front of me, I ran smack into a tree. Instead of helping me, the boy collapsed in laughter, unable to stop.

Summer in KTown wasn't complete without the ice cream truck. The moment we heard the carnival music of the truck coming down the street, we would race to find some loose change and dash to the truck. The line would be packed with kids shouting their orders. The taste of a cold bomb pop on a hot day was like a remedy to the hot sun.

The Fourth of July and New Year's brought fireworks—popping and sparkling in the night sky. We would set them on fire and then run. The entire street was alive with excitement as we celebrated together, the loud bangs echoing in the night air.

And then there were the water fights. We didn't have fancy pools or water parks, but we had something just as good—the fire hydrant. When it was opened, water sprayed everywhere, and we'd run through it in our T-shirts and shorts, laughing and splashing in the street. Or sometimes, we'd turn on the hosepipe and take turns getting drenched. That cool hose water was the best-tasting water there was, especially after hours of playing in the sun.

"It's my turn!" The next-in-line kid would say, ready to snatch the hose for a drink.

Our parents or the older kids would referee to make sure every kid got their share. "Wait, it's not your turn yet," they said, watching us with a smile as we kept running through the spray.

Those days in KTown were magical. Sure, there were spooky things that happened in that old apartment, but the fun we had—running through the streets, jumping off stairways and sliding boards, popping fireworks, and staying out late with friends—those memories are the ones that still make me smile.

What made those days so memorable wasn't the games or even the freedom. It was the sense of belonging to something greater–a community where everyone knew one another, children played carefree, and each day seemed like an adventure. Some of our most memorable moments were the evenings in KTown when the sun had already fallen, and we were still lost in laughter in the streets.

Insights from the Chapter: The Joy and Freedom of Childhood

This chapter is a vibrant reflection of childhood freedom, adventure, and the deep sense of community that defined life in KTown. While other parts of life may have had their challenges, the fun times in KTown were about pure, unfiltered joy—nights where kids ruled the streets, laughter echoed through the playgrounds, and adventure was waiting around every corner. Moments that taught me how to make the best of life's circumstances.

At the heart of it all was the playground, where impromptu baseball games turned everyday objects into bases, and daring jumps from slides and stairways made kids feel invincible. The thrill of testing limits—jumping from high places, leaping over thorny bushes, and racing bikes down hills—wasn't just about fun; it was about proving courage to each other and, most importantly, to themselves.

The chapter also captures the simplicity of childhood pleasures: picking fresh fruit from neighborhood trees, the rush of the ice cream truck's arrival, and the unbeatable taste of cool hose water on a hot day. Games like dodgeball, *Hide and Go Get*, and water fights with fire hydrants weren't just pastimes—they were traditions that bonded everyone together.

But beyond the games and excitement, the real magic of KTown was the sense of belonging. It was a place where kids could run free, where neighbors watched out for each other, and where every summer night felt endless. These weren't just moments of fun; they were the foundation of cherished memories, shaping the joy and resilience that would carry into adulthood.

Sixteen

The New Year's Eve Tragedy

It was New Year's Eve, and instead of hearing the usual laughter and music from the houses, the neighborhood was filled with the sound of sirens and whispers of shock. The news spread fast. A teenager, only 19 and pregnant, had been killed by her boyfriend. I remember when I first heard about the incident. Sitting on the porch, my friend Drea and I were trying to make sense of it all.

Talking in low voices, Drea's voice trembled as she asked, "Did you hear what happened to Angel?"

I nodded, feeling the tightening in my stomach and chest. "Yeah, I heard... her boyfriend shot her."

My friend repeated, "Shot her," like the words were stinging her tongue. "They said she was pregnant, innocently sitting in the car with him, her boyfriend." That wasn't fair to her. Trying to maintain a steady voice, I swallowed hard. "I heard he was playing around with the gun. That's what they're saying."

Drea shook her head, disbelief written all over her face. "Are you kidding? Playing with the gun? Why did he even point it at her? What type of game is that?"

I looked at the ground, feeling the weight of what happened. "They claimed she told him no... that she didn't want to do anything with him that night. That's when he threatened her with it."

My friend's eyes widened. "Because she said no?"

"Yeah," I replied quietly. "That's what I heard... that he panicked when the gun went off. Wrapped her in a rug and abandoned her behind the church, as if she were… nothing."

There was a long gap as we both tried to grasp the cruelty of it all. Drea clenched her fists, her eyes burning in anger.

"How could someone do that? She was pregnant. She had her entire life ahead of her, and now she's gone. Exactly like that."

I shook my head, and my throat tightened. "I do not know, Drea. I do not know."

We sat silently, the chilly air nipping at our skin. The celebration of New Year's Eve had been replaced by heavy, oppressive grief.

"I saw her just the other day, you know?" My friend spoke gently, hardly a whisper. "She was happy and talking about baby names. Now... now she's just... gone."

Tears welled up in my eyes, but I forced them down. "It's not fair."

"None of it is," My friend said, her voice tightening, holding in the sadness. "I just don't understand it. How could he? I mean, they were together... didn't he care about her at all?"

I didn't have an answer. I do not believe anyone did.

"They say he didn't mean to do it," I added, "That it was an accident." but that statement just didn't sound right. My friend scoffed.

"An accident? He aimed a gun at her. What did he think would happen?"

I shrugged. My heart felt heavy. "He was probably afraid. "He panicked, and then..."

My friend interrupted me with her sharp voice. "Scared? How about her? She must've been terrified."

I didn't know what else to say or think. We both sat there, the weight of the tragedy weighing heavily on us.

After a while, My friend let out a loud sigh. "Things like this shouldn't happen here. Not to people we know."

"No," I muttered. "But they do. It did."

The leaves rustled, and the wind whistled through the streets, carrying the weight of that night. We sat there, gazing out at the empty road, wondering how life could go on when something so careless had occurred so close to home.

My friend explained sadly, "She was only 19 years old," with a sad shake of her head. Like us, "She was still a child. And she's… gone now."

I wiped my eyes and nodded in amazement, my voice barely above a whisper, "Every New Year's Eve will be a memory of her. We have to remember her."

My friend answered, "We will," with a serene assurance in her voice. "We can't ever forget what happened to her."

And we didn't. The memory of Angel, the girl who was pregnant and murdered on New Year's Eve with hope for the future and was taken away too soon, would stay with us forever. She was a reminder of how sacred life is and how quickly it could be stolen from you, especially when you were just beginning to live it.

Insights from the Chapter: Memory, A Coping Mechanism

Grief has a way of settling into the corners of a community, reshaping the way people see the world. This chapter is a testament to the weight of loss, the cruelty of senseless violence, and the lasting echoes of tragedy. Angel, a young woman full of hope for the future, was taken in an instant—her life stolen by someone who was supposed to care for her. The shock of her murder ripples through me and Drea, forcing them to confront the harsh reality that safety is never guaranteed, not even in the places they call home.

At its core, this chapter explores the power of memory and the burden of injustice. Angel's death isn't just another crime in the news—it's personal. The way I and Drea wrestle with disbelief, anger, and sorrow reflects the helplessness that comes with trying to make sense of something so horrific. Emotionally, when we recall the memory of Angel, she will forever be 19 years old, and we will always feel like the children wounded by a peer's life that was stolen from us. And yet, amidst the pain, there is a quiet vow: to remember. Because remembering means refusing to let Angel become just another name lost to tragedy.

New Year's Eve is supposed to be a time of beginnings, but for us, every year, it became a reminder of all that was lost. Some wounds never truly heal, but in memory, Angel lives on.

Seventeen

Choosing Love in a World Where Hate Exists

In the summer of 1979, when I was just eight, the world I thought I knew began to change. Life in Morton Simpson Village, also known as Kingston, now called KTown, our close-knit neighborhood where everyone looked like me, had always felt sheltered. It was a place where kids played in the streets, mothers watched from doorways, and neighbors helped one another. I had learned about racism in history class and heard Martin Luther King's speeches on TV, but it all seemed like stories of the past—until that summer.

It started with the news of Bonita Carter's death. Bonita was a young Black woman who lived not far from my family's apartment in Kingston. At only twenty years old, she was shot by a white police officer, George Sands, outside Jerry's convenience store near her home. Bonita was trying to help a friend move his car. She was in the driver's seat when Officer Sands arrived at the scene. Without hesitation, he shot her at close range, taking her life in an instant.

The impact of her death spread through our community. Our parents talked about it, neighbors gathered outside, and tensions rose in ways I had never seen. I was just a child, but I knew something was deeply wrong. This wasn't just another story on the news—it was right here, in our world.

Fear swept through our community, especially when the Ku Klux Klan organization, clad in white robes and masks, came out to support the officer. They boldly rode through our neighborhood, defiantly parading their presence as a threat—stark, violent, and unyielding. They rode on horseback, their chants echoing through the streets, and it felt as if hatred had come alive. My mother gathered my siblings and me, pushing us quickly into a small closet. She hugged us tight just before shutting the door. I could feel her heartbeat pounding fast. She was afraid, and for the first time, so was I. It was a fear that was not like the usual childhood worries—it was the terror of being hated, of being unsafe, simply because of the color of our skin.

For the next three days, Kingston became a battleground of emotions. People marched, chanted, and demanded justice, their voices loud with pain and fury. Some of our neighbors, people who were usually calm and kind, seemed swept up in the energy of the moment. Their voices were now sharp with anger. It was like a black-and-white storm, and no one was left untouched. Sands, defended by the Fraternal Order of Police and the Klan, divided our city. And then there were distant gunshots, shouts, and the hum of helicopters. Even at my age, I understood that this was no ordinary summer.

The tension in our neighborhood entered every conversation, making our home feel unpleasant. Normally composed and steady, my mother kept us close under her while checking in with the neighbors and looking through the windows. My sheltered world had shattered in just a few days. I was beginning to understand that our skin color meant something to people outside our neighborhood, and that difference could bring out dangerous anger from those who didn't know us or care to know.

As a child, I wasn't raised with prejudice. I had teachers who were white, teachers who I trusted, loved, and learned from. They had shown me kindness, taught me to read and think, and praised me when I succeeded. To me, they were just people who helped me grow. So, even though the hatred from the racists that summer shook me, I knew better than to label every person based on those who caused us harm.

The memory of my teachers stayed with me as I tried to make sense of the anger and fear. In my youthful manner, I decided to choose love over hate at that moment. I would love anyone, regardless of skin color, who loved me and treated me with respect and care. What about those who didn't? I would just keep my distance, allowing their rage to burn out naturally without involving me.

That decision has stayed with me through life. Growing up in the shadow of Bonita Carter's death, I realized that the color of a person's skin could trigger hate in some, but it didn't have to define who I chose to welcome into my life. That summer taught me that we live in a world where both love and hate exist, and it's up to us to choose which one will shape our lives.

Insights from the Chapter: Defined by Choice

Hate is a learned behavior, but so is love. This chapter explores the moment that I, as an innocent child, first encountered the weight of racism—not through textbooks or distant stories but in my own neighborhood, where life had once felt safe and familiar. It captures the heartbreak of realizing that not everyone sees you as simply a child, but as a threat, an enemy, or less than human.

The tragic death of Bonita Carter shattered the illusion of safety in Kingston, turning a peaceful community into a place of fear, anger, and division. It was not just about a single act of violence—it was about a system that allowed it, defended it, and even celebrated it. The sight of the Ku Klux Klan riding through the neighborhood, their presence meant to intimidate, exposed a chilling truth: hatred was not a relic of the past, but a force still thriving in the present.

Yet, even in the face of such deep-rooted hatred, I make a powerful choice—to embrace love. I refused to let the actions of the hateful define how I see the world. Instead of mirroring their anger, I choose to consider people by their character, not their skin color. That moment of clarity, born from fear and uncertainty, becomes a guiding principle for life.

This chapter is a reminder that both love and hate shape the world, but we each have the power to decide which one we will carry forward.

Eighteen

The Gift of Song

Kingston projects had a lot of commotion, like children laughing, people conversing, and the police sirens due to the crime. However, music was the only sound that anchored my best friend and me. Not just any music, though; it was the tunes we all sang in the church choir, which served as both our haven and a means of escape from the outside world. The youth choir was a joy to hear and watch. The choir director, Majer, stood in front, performing and directing like a conductor leading a symphony as the children sang in harmony.

Looking back, I realized music was woven into my family's story long before I ever stood on that choir stage. My great-grandfather, a jazz band leader, was famous in his own right. He played the trombone with a passion that brought his music to life, each note a part of him. People still talked about him, his trombone filling the streets on warm evenings and the way his melodies made people feel alive. He made such an impact on music that he was honored in a book written in the 1950s by Frederic Ramsey, Jr. called "Been Here and Gone" about African American music in the South.

But it wasn't just him. My great-grandmother, grandmother, and my mother all had voices that could make you feel something powerful. Every Sunday morning, they filled the house with praise and worship, singing gospel tunes as they prepared for church. No matter how bad things got outside, my mother's voice, which was passed down from the matriarchs of our family, had a way of making you feel better. Her songs filled our house with a warmth that was unbreakable. As a child, I learned that music wasn't just sound; it was comfort, strength, and a bond that ran through my family's very DNA.

At just eight years old, I hadn't yet realized how music would shape me. It was Sharin who nudged me into the choir. She'd joined a few weeks before and couldn't stop talking about it.

"You've got to come to practice," she urged one evening as we sat on my front porch. "Majer teaches the choir how to sing unlike any teacher at school and not like any other choir director. He's… fun. Plus, you can sing."

I rolled my eyes, pretending to brush it off. "Me? Sing? I don't know about that."

"No way! I've heard you sing," she said, grinning. "You've got a voice. Trust me."

The next week, I found myself standing in the back row of the choir, feeling both excited and terrified. Majer, our choir director, was like no one I'd ever met. He wasn't just waving his hands and telling us to sing louder; he brought the music to life, guiding us through each harmony like a maestro. He broke down the voice parts—Soprano, Alto, Tenor, and Bass—making each feel essential, like pieces of a grand puzzle.

He clapped his hands and smiled when he saw me on my first practice. "Ah, a new voice! Come on up here. Let's see what you've got."

I paused, feeling anxious. Sharin gave me a push, and I took a step forward. Something changed inside of me as we started singing. All I could hear was our voices rising as one as the entire world went away. In addition to the choir, I felt a connection to something more profound that spanned my family's generations. At that moment, I understood that music was more than simply a sound; it was a fit that had been given to me and something I was destined to preserve.

Majer came over and put a hand on my shoulder after practice. "You did good," he said with warm encouragement. "Keep at it."

"Thank you. I will." I smiled, a feeling of pride warming my chest.

I started to count down the days until choir practice as time went on. Inside that church, surrounded by music, I felt safe, even though the area could be wild at any time, with fights breaking out and sirens ringing. Still feeling high from choir practice, Sharin and I would talk for hours about our dreams, how Majer made us feel like professional singers, and how our minister had a voice that seemed to reach the stars.

Sharin and I sat on the church steps one Sunday after the service. My eyes were full of appreciation as I said, "Did you hear Rev today?" She laughed, "How could I miss it? He seems to be able to perform without a microphone."

"Right? And Majer… he makes us sound like a real choir, not just a bunch of kids," she exclaimed with a big smile.

I glanced down the street, looking past our wild neighborhood. "It's not just about singing, you know? It makes everything feel lighter."

Sharin nodded, her expression becoming serious. "It helps. It gives us a sense of belonging."

In that church choir, I discovered a voice that was more than just mine—it was the voice of my family, a history founded on love, tenacity, and an understanding that music could brighten even the darkest days. I felt my great-grandfather's trombone, my mother and grandmother's harmonies combining with mine, and the deep faith that carried us all. During the chaos, the songs we sang gave me strength and helped me stay centered.

I turned to Sharin one Sunday with a lot of feelings after a particularly meaningful sermon. Quietly, I confessed, "I don't know what I'd do without this choir." "Neither do I," she said, her eyes displaying the same appreciation. "It keeps us out of trouble, sort of."

I nodded. I knew exactly what she meant. Music was more than simply a hobby; it was our means of survival and a haven from a sometimes harsh and noisy outside world. And through the music, with Sharin by my side and Majer leading the way, I found my voice—a voice that would carry me forward, no matter where life took me. The gift of song wasn't just something I inherited; it was something I was living every day, a legacy I would carry with me always.

Insights from the Chapter: Finding a Voice

Music has the power to heal, unite, and provide a sense of purpose. This chapter captures the transformative role of music in my life, revealing how it became a source of refuge, strength, and identity in a world that often felt chaotic.

Growing up in Kingston, where the sounds of laughter, conversations, and police sirens filled the air, the music stood apart. It wasn't just entertainment—it was a sanctuary. Church choir practice was more than a weekly gathering; it was a place of belonging, discipline, and joy. Under Majer's guidance, the choir wasn't just about singing—it was about creating something greater than themselves.

My deep-rooted connection to music wasn't accidental—it was woven into the fabric of family history. With a great-grandfather who led a jazz band and generations of women who filled their homes with gospel songs, music wasn't just a talent; it was an inheritance. But it wasn't until my best friend's encouragement led me to join the choir that I realized music wasn't just in the family—it was in me.

Stepping into that church, I found more than a melody; I found confidence and purpose. The choir wasn't just a group of kids—it was a lifeline, a place where voices blended into something powerful. The outside world, with its dangers and uncertainties, couldn't reach us when we sang. In those moments, music became a shield, a source of light in the darkness. Through choir practices, friendships, and Sunday services, I learned that music wasn't just about sound—it was about connection, faith, and survival. It was a gift, not just to be received but to be carried forward, shaping my journey for years to come.

Nineteen

Fashion, Faith, and Keeping Up

KTown was full of unique personalities and no place was that more visible than at First Baptist Kingston Church on Sundays. Youth Day was especially memorable. On those days, the children filled the choir stand while young adults and other children sat proudly in the audience.

Everyone wore their Sunday best, but some people stood out. Some folks knew how to really dress, coordinating outfits in ways no one would expect, mixing prints and bold colors effortlessly. You'd see mink coats, sharp suits, and elegant church hats.

Somebody would say, "Ooooh, look at Sister!" and nudge the person next to them. "She did match the leopard print and stripes, and it looks good!"

It was always something special when the young girls came in wearing their own church hats, just like the older women.

"Girl, look at that hat!" The girl beamed, tilting her head just enough for the sequins to catch the light.

"You fancy now!" her friend giggled. "You better not let it fall off when we shout."

There were men and women, young and old, and then there were the shouters. One young woman, in particular, was unforgettable. She would shout, sing, play the tambourine, dance up and down the aisles, and eventually pass out in the spirit.

"There she goes!" someone whispered as the tambourine started up.

"Three… two… and she was gone!" another kid called, just as the young woman twirled and fell gently into a waiting usher's arms.

The children across the sanctuary watched with wide eyes, some in awe, some trying not to laugh too loud. They were always keeping track of the most memorable characters in the room.

And then came the sleepy moments. The Reverend's sermons were strong, but his voice sometimes put the elders straight into a slumber.

"Look at Deacon sleep again," a boy nudged the kid next to him.

"He got that holy nap going!" the kids chuckled, watching one of the deacons gently nod off on stage.

Youth Day also meant youth musicians and youth preachers. The young musicians would sneak in riffs and rhythms from familiar R&B songs.

"Wait… was that Prince?" one of the children would say.

"That was definitely Prince!" the kids in the sanctuary laughed. "They bold!"

And nobody got left behind at First Baptist. Children with special needs were placed front and center to lead prayer, speak, or sing solo.

They were always welcome to do more, signaled by loud "Amens!" and clapping from the congregation.

"Go ahead, baby!" someone would shout from the back as a young boy nervously read his scripture.

"Take your time, now!" the choir director would say, smiling wide.

"You are doing just fine!" the deacons echoed in unison.

With all that going on, church was more than just a service. It was laughter and encouragement, fashion and rhythm, praise and pride. It was a sanctuary that lifted our spirits, a safe space from the struggles of poverty and the daily challenges we faced in the neighborhood.

Insights from the Chapter: Therapy from Church

Church life in KTown wasn't just a place of worship; it was a place for identity, expression, and belonging. Sunday Service was transformed into a celebration of resilience and joy through the expression of fashion, music, tradition, and laughter. The moments shared between the children conversing and playful teasing show how cultural memories are created in places like First Baptist Kingson. Even in the face of poverty and struggle, this chapter is about how community and faith can be sources of light, humor, and hope, especially for the young, who watched and learned what it meant to belong, to believe, and to be seen.

Twenty

Claimed in KTown

One summer afternoon, my friend Sharin and I were outside, jumping, running, and losing ourselves, playing our childhood games. The heat waves were visual, and the air was thick with laughter, dust, and the smell of freshly cut grass. Then we noticed my Kingston Elementary classmate Beau and another boy making their way up the street toward us, swaggering a bit as only nine-year-old boys could. Beau, with his significant cowboy walk and his friend, had hypnotizing eyes that became more mesmerizing in the light.

As he came closer and nodded at us, Beau smiled. He cried out, “Hey, Faithe!” over the noise of our laughter. “Who is your friend?

“This is Sharin,” I said with a bashful smile.

With a head turn, Beau pointed to the boy next to him. “Well, this is my friend Rico from another neighborhood. Y’all got boyfriends yet?”

Sharin and I exchanged a look and burst into laughter. Boyfriends? We were nine, after all! But Beau’s question sent a thrill through us, the kind that made us feel older like we were part of some grand, grown-up game.

Beau took our laughter as a good sign, nodding seriously. “Alright, then. Faithe, since I already know you, Sharin will be my girlfriend, and Rico can be yours. That way, we both get to know someone new. Faithe, we see each other every day at school, anyway," he added with a grin.

Sharin and I exchanged wide-eyed looks and tried to contain our laughter, but the idea was too funny and sweet. We nodded, barely holding back giggles as we all pretended, just for a moment, that these titles meant something more than a game.

"Guess that makes us official, huh, Faithe?" Rico said, trying to sound serious.

I blushed, looking down, trying not to be mesmerized by his eyes while tracing my shoe in the dirt. "Yeah, I guess so."

"What do you wanna do, Faithe?" Rico said.

The whole thing was so innocent, so far removed from the real world around us. Just two boy kids "claiming" two girls for the day, all of us running through yards, playing hide and seek, and racing down the sidewalks until dark began to settle.

Sharin I laughed so hard that we could be heard down the street. "Do you believe that we are now officially girlfriends?" With a cheeky sparkle in her eye, she whispered.

I replied in a low voice, "I guess so," and we both started laughing again, the innocence of it all giving us butterflies I've only ever experienced as a child. We continued outside, laughing and running, allowing the mere fact that two males in the area had declared us "girlfriends" to hold us in the magic of that day.

While that day in KTown felt like the beginning of something new, a giddy experiment in being "claimed," I already knew a little about the feeling of connection, however innocent it was. Both memories live side by side with what young love looked like in its earliest, most unfiltered forms.

Insights from the Chapter: Innocent Love

This chapter reminds me of how innocent childhood love can shape understanding of connection. Sharin and I were nine years old and carefree. She and I were swept up in a bigger moment than our small world. Beau and Rico claimed us as their girlfriends. That was a moment of excitement of being seen, noticed, and chosen. It wasn't love the way adults understand it, but it was a good feeling and a sense of belonging.

The magic of the moment wasn't in the title of being "girlfriends." It was the innocence of it all. It was the thrill of being part of something new, of playing pretend, and feeling, for the briefest moment, like we were stepping into a world we didn't fully understand but were eager to explore. There was nothing more to it, just a pure connection between two girls and two boys who didn't know any better than to simply enjoy the moment for what it was.

My first connection that actually happened in kindergarten was simple and innocent. It wasn't about romantic love; it was about feeling seen, about a quiet bond that made me feel safe. And that's what I realize now. Whether I was age five or nine, the concept was the same. Love, in its truest form, is not complicated or defined. Innocent experiences can teach us something profound about connection. Those early moments of connection set the stage for how we understand love later in life.

Twenty-One

Showdown In KTown

There are many stories in KTown; some of the most memorable stories linger, like the ones where a single, terrible choice forever changes lives. One such story belonged to a man in our neighborhood, a man whose life and actions served as a warning about the dark intersections of fear, betrayal, and regret.

This man, let's call him Tim, was known around the neighborhood as a participant in many social events but kept mostly to himself. He had a calm presence. He wasn't one to start fights, but he carried a gun. He wasn't a fighter and was known to have behavior that made people want to fight him, but he couldn't fight, so his gun was his protection.

Tim was a nice dresser, attractive, and envied by many. He began an affair with Rip's wife. Rip was a tall and big man who loved his wife and family. Rip was the kind of person who respected everyone and maintained his family as the top priority. He loved his wife deeply, in the sort of way that made people see him as almost naive. It seemed he trusted her and assumed their bond was strong enough to keep her close. But innocence and good intentions often collide with harsh reality, and one night, Rip finds out the truth.

Tension had been building for weeks before it exploded that night. Rip walked up to attempt to confront Tim, standing in his position and protecting his family, honor, and pride. He may have thought that Tim would be convinced to change his mind by the truth and the principles of it all. But Tim, seeing Rip's anger, felt cornered and exposed. And that fear, that twisted instinct for survival, took over. Before he could even think, Tim pulled the gun from his pocket and fired. In a showdown, Rip's weapon was his size, while Tim's defense was his gun. The gun that won the fight and ended a life.

In an instant, the whole neighborhood was shaken. There lay a guy who had done nothing but stand up for his family. As though the air itself was holding its breath, there was silence. Even the children who received the news the following day felt the ground move beneath them, their conception of safety shaken by the weight of Tim's anxiety, which had claimed an innocent life.

The aftermath, however, was worse. Like wildfire, whispers spread around KTown, each one adding layers of remorse, grief, and rage while also slightly altering the narrative. People believed Rip just wanted to chat and regain Tim's dignity and hadn't done him any harm. However, Tim had anticipated the worst and believed Rip would hit him or, at least, publicly humiliate him. Tim decided he would never be able to reverse in that moment of terror.

Some said Tim wasn't just defending himself that night; a twisted sense of pride and desperation drove him. But the courts saw it differently. His lawyer argued it was self-defense that Tim had felt trapped and acted on instinct, protecting himself against a man he claimed was aggressive. And somehow, his crime was dismissed as "justifiable," and he was allowed to go free.

However, that didn't seem reasonable to some in the neighborhood. Tim's guilt could not be erased in a courtroom. A guy had died, his family had dispersed, and the question of what motivated someone to commit homicide hovered over us. We learned that panic could enter our souls and make even decent people act strangely, shattering families and taking lives because of a little instant when fear takes over.

After that, Tim didn't talk to many people. He kept his head down and stayed out of sight as much as possible. But the shadow of his actions continued to haunt the place where the incident occurred, reminding us that terror can drown innocence.

Insights from the Chapter: The Cost of Fear

This chapter reminds me of how somethings stay with you, not because you want them to, but because they change the way you see the world. What happened between Tim and Rip in KTown was one of those things. I lived through that time, which taught me one of the hardest truths: fear has a cost.

Rip deserved better. He didn't come after Tim looking for a fight. He came for truth and to defend his name and his home, like anyone who loved their spouse would.

Tim let fear take over. Instead of facing Rip with honesty or humility, he reached for what made him feel safe: that gun. Then, in a flash of panic, he pulled the trigger.

Rip was gone.

It was called self-defense by law. Fear pulled the trigger. Not reason. Not necessity. Fear. It had cost a life that was just as deserving as any other. A father. A husband. A neighbor.

Tim didn’t go to prison, but he didn’t walk away free either. He carried the weight of it all in his eyes. He changed his lifestyle and decision process from that point on. He may not have been behind bars, but he was living a different kind of sentence. The kind where you can't run from what you did, even if the law says you can.

That incident taught me something I’ll never forget: fear can move you before you have a chance to think. The damage it leaves behind can be permanent. You can apologize for mistakes. You can rebuild trust. But, some losses are deep and final.

Fear cost Tim his peace. It cost Rip his life. And it cost the community its belief in safety and what’s right.

I’ve learned since then to listen to fear but not obey it. Because when fear is in control, nobody wins. Sometimes, the cost is more than we can bear. And sometimes, when we switch the story it hits even harder. Imagine if it were two women and a man, if one woman took another woman’s life over the man they both loved. Would we see it differently? Would we understand fear in the same way? Love? Possession? Loss? The story doesn’t change, but how we see it just might.

Twenty-Two

Losing Ground

We rarely ate out, and we never purchased sweets since, Mother always kept a stock of sugar, eggs, butter, flour, and spices. We used items from our pantry to make our own baked goods from scratch.

Being a devout woman, my mother taught us the value of prayer and religion. She even admitted at one point that she had thought about becoming a nun. Many said that she had a unique spiritual skill since she could decipher dreams and foretell future occurrences in other people's lives. When I was five years old, I had a dream that she translated and frequently told me about.

Sadly, a tragedy that occurred to her changed everything. This, in my opinion, was an attack on her, meant to drive her from her faith and cause others to believe she was insane, thereby separating them from her and her spiritual gift.

The day my mother lost her job marked a turning point in our lives that I hadn't anticipated. She'd been the foundation of our family, the steady, vibrant spirit who kept us going. But that spirit seemed to fade after she came home with her final paycheck. I could see her strength declining a little more each moment. Her once-constant laughing faded, giving way to sighs and times when she would nod off and lose herself in her thoughts. First, confusion, then despair. The mother I knew started to disappear, and eventually, the residents of

KTown muttered and called her "crazy," her spirit being broken piece by piece by the silent scars of a thousand small heartbreaks.

In retrospect, I can see that my mother's hardships were caused by a lifetime of losses that eroded her fortitude, not just one job. She was nearing the end of her joyful reign through KTown, the neighborhood she had lived in for decades. The neighborhood, which was previously filled with people and experiences she treasured, seemed to be slipping away.

The first tragedy happened when I was five. Her older brother, my uncle, passed away in a tragic car accident. He'd been terrified of 18-wheelers, and one rainy day, that fear met him head-on. His car lost control next to one of those massive trucks, and he was crushed in his car. It was one of my earliest memories of loss, though, at the time, I was too young to understand what death meant. But I sensed my mother's sorrow, even in her attempts to shield me from it. I saw the way she held back tears, the way she gripped my hand just a little tighter.

The years went on, but the losses didn't stop. When I was nine, my mother's best friend, practically a sister to her, passed away suddenly during childbirth. It was another blow, taking from her someone she'd leaned on, confided in, and laughed with. The loss felt unbearable, and though I didn't fully grasp it then, I saw my mother's grief deepen. Just a year later, she suffered another heartbreak when her last pregnancy ended in miscarriage, a trauma that led to surgery ensuring she'd never have another child. I remember, years later, when she told me how her heart broke that day. She'd wanted a big family.

She'd said, "I wanted more children, and they took that away from me at the hospital." She wanted a full house bustling with kids. That dream was destroyed.

Another tragedy struck close to home when I started high school. A sudden brain aneurysm claimed the life of my mother's fiancé, a man who had promised her a fresh start and loved her. Her heart hurt even more, grieving after his death, and she became a more withdrawn person who lived her life as though she were only partially there. Then, just a year later, when I was fourteen, my grandmother passed away from cancer. Then, the next year, my brother began his prison sentence. It was as if that final loss took what little resolve my mother had left.

I watched my mother begin to change after the loss of my grandmother gradually. She was coming to terms with where the sorrow she had experienced began to characterize her. By the time my mother was in her fifties, it seemed as if she thought her own life was coming to an end, just as my grandmother had died at sixty-three. She seemed to be counting down the days until her passing since she was nearing the same age as when my grandmother's life abruptly ended. She began to talk about seeing her mother again and the day she would meet the same ending and sing gospel songs about when she would cross "the pearly gates" as when her mother had passed.

She started wearing moo-moo house dresses, the kind of clothes that older women in our neighborhood wore when they were ready to slow down and rest. Her demeanor softened, took on the gentleness of age, and she carried herself as though preparing for something beyond my understanding. She'd express how much she missed her mother. At times, she would even cry, and I'd see the longing in her eyes as if the years since my grandmother's passing had only deepened her realization of the love they had shared. She would talk about her mother with a tenderness that revealed regrets—regrets for moments she wished she could have shown her appreciation for the words left unspoken.

In those moments, it felt as if my mother was trying to reach across time to heal that part of her heart. My grandmother had been a woman of unwavering faith, always praying and singing gospel songs. I remember those melodies from my childhood, my grandmother's voice rising in gentle reverence, each note a prayer for her children and grandchildren. In her grief, my mother hummed those old gospel songs around the house, carrying forward the love and faith she had inherited. It was her way of keeping her mother close, her way of honoring the woman who had shaped her.

Her grief became a quiet rhythm in our lives, a bittersweet tribute that I came to recognize as a mother's enduring love. Every song and silent prayer served as a link between the past and the present, reminding me of my mother's resilience even in her most vulnerable moments. I realized at the time that her grief was not merely a way for her to vent her anguish but rather a reflection of the love she still had for her mother, a love that became a part of who she was and her means of clinging to the person she missed so much.

I didn't fully understand the weight of her grief until I left home. At twenty, I packed my bags, pregnant and married, left the orange brick projects behind and set out for California with my husband at the age of twenty. I remember the look on her face, a mixture of pride and heartbreak. She said to me, with tears in her eyes, "You just want to leave me." At the time, I couldn't understand why she made my choice feel so personal. I was an adult, ready to live my own life, but I see now that my leaving was another fracture in her heart, another person she'd cherished slipping out of reach.

As time went on, my sister started telling me things that worried me. She said Mama was acting strange, saying things that didn't make sense, like she was talking to people who weren't there. She blamed it on a trip to a holiness church, claiming my mother had come back possessed by strange spirits. I didn't believe her. But a few years later, life took me back home, and I began to see what my sister had meant. My mother would wander through rooms, murmuring rhyming words, chanting prayers, and speaking in tongues, her mind somewhere far away. Her brilliant words, inspiration, and advice were becoming confusing. It was as though she were adrift, lost in a sea of memories and sorrows.

Over the course of ten years, her condition worsened. Without a job, she couldn't afford the rent, and eventually, she lost the apartment in KTown that had been our home. It seemed that as she left KTown, so too did the last threads of stability in her life. She became a figure that people in the neighborhood watched with pity, whispering about her as she wandered, clutching onto pieces of a life that was slowly slipping away.

In a way, KTown was leaving her, but I don't think KTown ever really let her go. It felt like the place had cast a kind of spell on her as if the pain and sorrow she'd endured there had taken root too deeply ever to be fully shaken. She wasn't the only one, either; others in KTown seemed lost, consumed by their struggles and heartbreaks. In that neighborhood, it felt like people lost themselves in ways I couldn't explain—worn down by life, by loss, by the weight of dreams that never came true.

Looking back, I can see that my mother's decline wasn't abrupt. No one could have survived the gradual disintegration and accumulation of losses without suffering scars. Nevertheless, I held onto the memories of the mother she used to be, even at her worst hours. The mother who taught me faith and resiliency, who loved her family with all of her heart. Even though she lost her ground, she gave me seeds that will endure long after the pains of KTown are forgotten.

Insights from the Chapter: Grief Response and Role Reassignment

This chapter is a personal example of grief, resilience, and the slow unraveling of a woman who once stood as the rock of her family. It traces the life of my mother, a woman of faith and strength who faced a series of devastating losses that slowly chipped away at her spirit.

Her faith was once unwavering, a force that guided her and those around her. But life in KTown, marked by tragedies both personal and communal, took its toll. The loss of her brother, best friend, unborn child, fiancé, and mother, then the imprisonment of my brother—her son weighed on her, each death leaving an invisible scar. The pain was cumulative, and with every heartbreak, she withdrew further into herself. When she lost her job, it marked more than a financial crisis—it symbolized the final unraveling of a woman who had already lost so much.

As she grew older, it felt as if she was preparing for her own passing. She sang gospel songs in remembrance of her mother and carried her grief as a quiet but ever-present burden. My sister and I watched her slip away, first emotionally, then physically, as she lost her home and became a shadow of the woman she once was.

This chapter serves as a powerful reflection on how loss, when left unhealed, can consume a person. Yet, beyond the sorrow, finding a lasting gift—the strength and faith my mother instilled in us, resilience that continues to grow beyond the tragedies we experienced in KTown. My mother was once the pillar of her family. She was a woman of faith, strength, and determination. Then the roles reversed where she went from the nurturing one to the one who needed to be cared for by her daughters. Despite the sorrow we experienced, the resilience and faith instilled in us allowed us to step up and become what we needed to be to create new means of hope and stability.

Twenty-Three

Loyalty is Everything

Loyalty plays a key role in KTown. The bonds that tie individuals together often remain unseen until controversy arises. When loyalty is present, the arguments, heartaches, and betrayals all become less significant. People argue, but they want to remain friends. They will occasionally even pardon the unforgivable.

I vividly recall a story that exemplifies the depth of this loyalty. It was about two women, Pat and Jody, who were best friends and neighbors as children. They had played together since they were young and had a bond like sisters.

Pat was the first to get married, tying the knot with Brice, a well-liked man in the neighborhood. For fifteen years, they seemed happy, but slowly, cracks began to form, and their marriage began to fade. After a decade and a half, their marriage ended. I remember seeing Pat not long after it happened.

One Sunday, as we stood outside the church, she shrugged and remarked, "It just wasn't working anymore. But it's alright. Things change."

Unsure of what to say, I nodded. "Yeah, but after all those years, it must be tough."

Despite her smile, Pat's eyes were sorrowful. "Yes, it is. But, you know what? Brice and I are still friends. Life goes on."

No one thought much of it at the time. Divorce happens. People drift apart. But what came next truly shocked everyone.

A year or so later, Jody, Pat's playmate since childhood, married Brice.

I remember the beginning of the rumors. People were surprised. "Did you hear?" Mrs. Robinson whispered to my mother One afternoon, "Jody married someone."

"That's great," Mama remarked. "To whom?"

"Pat's ex-husband!" Mrs. Robinson said.

"What?" My mom let out a gasp. "After all of the things he and Pat have experienced together?"

The neighborhood buzzed with speculation. Some questioned Pat's reaction, while others claimed it was a betrayal. But when Sunday came around, and we all saw them at church—Pat, Jody, and Brice—the tension we expected never existed.

Pat approached Jody and spoke to them nicely at church service, "Hi Brice and Jody, how is y'all doing?" Her voice was steady, and her expressions were unreadable.

Jody blinked as if surprised by the kindness in Pat's voice.

From that moment on, things were... well, different, but they weren't hostile. Jody and Pat didn't cut each other off. They still spoke when they saw each other and still greeted each other at church.

Then, years later, Pat passed away. When I saw Jody and Brice standing together at her funeral, I couldn't help but feel a wave of emotion. It was strange, but in their own way, they were honoring Pat despite everything. There they were, paying their respects after everything that had transpired. As we walked out of the church that day, Jody was crying, and her eyes were red. "We were family, even when things got complicated."

This was the way KTown operated. Big, showy acts weren't always the hallmark of loyalty. It was about maintaining relationships even when life threw curveballs. No matter what stood in their way, people here had a way of sticking together.

Insights from the Chapter: Resilient Ties

True loyalty isn't about big, dramatic gestures—it's about sticking by people even when life gets messy. In KTown, friendships and relationships don't just fall apart because of change or hardship. People find ways to stay connected, even when things don't turn out the way they expected.

Pat and Jody's story is a perfect example. Pat was married to Brice for fifteen years, but when their marriage ended, she didn't hold onto bitterness. No one thought much of it at the time—divorces happen. But when Jody, Pat's childhood best friend, ended up marrying Brice, people assumed it would cause a rift. Instead, Pat surprised everyone. She didn't lash out or cut Jody off. When she saw them at church, she greeted them like nothing had changed.

The neighborhood talked, wondering if Pat felt betrayed, but she never showed anger. Life moved on. Even at Pat's funeral years later, Jody and Brice stood together, mourning her. At that moment, it was clear—despite everything, they were still family.

This is a reminder that loyalty isn't always loud. It's not about proving a point or making a scene. It's about choosing to hold onto relationships, even when they don't look the way they used to. In KTown, people don't let life's twists and turns break their bonds. They find a way to stay together.

Twenty-Four

The Village That Raised Us

When we were kids growing up, it felt like we were living in a village. Every adult looked out for every child, and no one's business was truly private. You couldn't get away with much because if one adult didn't see you, another one would. The streets were filled with familiar faces, and everyone felt like family.

I'll never forget the time I snuck a boy into the house. My mother wasn't home, but the lady from next door saw everything. She didn't say a word to me at the moment, but I knew she'd tell my mother as soon as she got home.

With a cunning grin, the neighbor told her, "Yep, she had a boy in the house while you were at work." Listening from around the corner, my heart sank. I prepared myself for a scolding when my mother entered. I stumbled, "Uh… Mama, he was just bringing me my book from school."

"A book?" she asked, raising an eyebrow in response. I tried not to show my nervousness by nodding. She studied my face for a moment, then, to my surprise, gave me a knowing smile. "He just brought your book from school, then?"

"Yes, Mama! I really needed it to finish my homework." A sense of relief swept over me. Her face softened as she sighed. "Well, you have my trust. You've always done your homework well, and I do not doubt that you wouldn't allow anyone to divert you from your goals," replied Mama. I appreciated her trust. There was no getting away with anything in our neighborhood since someone was always watching.

The kids in KTown would always jump the fences to pick figs and pecans from our neighbors' yards, believing we were clever little thieves.

"You think we can make it?" I asked one day, glancing over the fence at the towering trees heavy with ripe fruit.

"Sure can!" My friend Emgee, who was already climbing the fence, advised me just to go over and get a few.

We jumped over to the opposite side while our hearts raced. We were giddy with excitement as soon as we stepped into Mrs. Lawson's yard. With its limbs heavy with juicy, sun-warmed fruit, we hurried toward the closest fig tree.

"Take a look at those figs!" I exclaimed, reaching out to pluck one. I took a large mouthful, letting the juice run down my fingers. "This is amazing!"

"Grab more quickly!" Emgee yelled, with his pockets already stuffed full of fruit. Meanwhile, another friend hurried to the pecan tree, shaking its limbs and watching the nuts fall like treasure.

Just as we were enjoying our stolen feast, a feeling of unease crept over me. It was too still, too silent. All of a sudden, I saw an adult standing on the porch of a house next door, watching us. When I recognized Mr. Whis, the elderly man who lived next door, my heart dropped. He yelled across the yard, "Get down from there and get home before I tell your mama what you've been up to!"

We both looked at each other frantically as panic swept through us. "Run!" I shouted, dropping the half-eaten fig and sprinting back toward the fence.

We scrambled over the fence. Just as I was about to leap back to safety, I heard Mr. Whis's voice call out behind us. "You kids better not think you're getting away with this!"

We didn't stop to respond. By the time we reached the other side, we were breathless and wide-eyed, hearts pounding like drums in our chests. But as we reached the safety of our yard, we couldn't help but laugh, even as fear tinged our voices.

It was not long before the news traveled back home. Our parents were already aware of the situation. The entire block seemed to be watching, and the community had a way of keeping kids in line.

Even though I could see a little smile teasing her lips, my mother cautioned, "You all better be careful next time. Stealing fruit isn't the way to go."

We nodded, our laughter fading but the thrill of our little adventure still buzzing in our minds. We may have gotten caught, but it didn't take away the fun we had—or the memories we made sneaking around in search of sweet treasures.

But it wasn't just about discipline. The adults in KTown protected us, too. If someone's car broke down, you'd see neighbors giving rides. If an elderly neighbor were struggling to carry groceries, some teenagers would rush over to help.

"I got it, Miss Mae," I remember hearing Emgee say one day, running across the street to help our elderly neighbor with her bags. "Let me take that for you."

It wasn't just kindness. It was loyalty—a sense of duty to one another. We respected and looked out for the elderly because it was ingrained in us. Even the elders respected one another, greeting them as "ma'am" or "sir." In KTown, the elders were the heartbeat of the community, the living memory of where we'd come from. Taking care of them wasn't just a chore—it was an honor.

There's a certain peace in knowing that no matter what happens, the people around you will stand by you. KTown was far from perfect, but its loyalty—deep-rooted, almost stubborn—held everything together. Even though we had disagreements and made mistakes with our playmates, we always ended up getting back together.

In KTown, loyalty never wavered. Somehow, the bonds that held us together remained intact even when life changed, even when friendships were tested. No matter the cost, we managed to stay faithful. And it was all that mattered in KTown.

Insights from the Chapter: Trust, Loyalty and Discipline

KTown was a tight-knit community where everyone looked out for each other. In KTown, raising kids wasn't just a job for parents—it was a responsibility shared by the whole neighborhood. Privacy was rare, but that also meant you always had someone watching your back.

The story about sneaking a boy into the house highlights the way trust works. My mother didn't explode in anger; she tested my honesty. It wasn't just about discipline—it was about building character and reinforcing the idea that trust is earned, not given.

The fig-stealing adventure displays how childhood was full of small mischiefs, but even then, the adults made sure kids stayed in line. The community didn't just discipline—it protected. Whether it was scolding a kid for climbing fences or helping an elderly neighbor with groceries, people in KTown took care of one another.

The chapter also emphasizes loyalty—not just between friends but within the entire community. Respect for elders wasn't optional; it was ingrained. Even when kids got into trouble, there was an understanding that they were still part of something bigger.

Ultimately, a sense of belonging is the essence of what made KTown special: a sense of belonging. Even when life got messy, relationships stayed intact. No matter what, people stood by each other—and that's what truly mattered.

Twenty-Five

KTOWN for Life

Driving through the streets of my old neighborhood to take my aunt home, It had been years since I walked these blocks, but everything felt just the same. The sidewalks still looked the same but a little worn with grassroots coming out of them. I could hear the sound of people laughing and drinking outside, and I could almost picture my childhood friends and our younger selves playing there again.

As I turned the corner, my aunt said, "Do you remember him?" She pointed ahead. He just recently returned home. I saw him walking up and down the street getting in exercise —Beau, my elementary school classmate and friend from childhood. He had aged gracefully, now an older version of the young guy I remembered: his head shaved bald with a gray beard framing his face, a charming smile, and that spark in his eyes that always meant fun was nearby.

"Beau!" I stopped the car, got out, and shouted, waving my arm.

He looked up, and his face lit up with joy as he said my childhood name. "Ms. Cooper! Oh wow! It's been so long!"

We were hugging tightly before I even realized it. We both smiled as if we had discovered a hidden gem as we took a step back.

"Isn't it unbelievable that we're back here?" I asked with excitement. "It's like we never left!"

Beau stared at me and said, “You look exactly the same as you did back then!” his eyes gleamed.

“Remember the times we had at Kingston Elementary?”

I laughed. “I remember those lunchroom cinnamon rolls that the lady sold at her house near us.”

“She stayed in the back of your grandmother. She sold the cinnamon rolls for 50 cents,” replied Beau.

“Do you remember how tough it was sometimes?” I asked, my voice growing serious. Like the days when fights broke out every day after school?

Beau gave a nod. “Yes, but I had your back. Nobody could harm you without me stepping in.”

“And I had your back.” “Being loyal meant everything,” I stated with pride.

“Even when things got rough, we stood by each other.”

“And respect,” added Beau. “We learned to stand up for one another.”

“In KTOWN, we looked out for each other. I’ll never forget that,” I said, feeling a sense of pride in our special place.

Beau smiled brightly. “KTOWN for life!” he said, lifting his hand in the air and signing the letter ‘K’ in sign language.

I laughed and raised my own hand, making the letter ‘K’ with my fingers.” KTOWN!” I replied. At that moment, we felt like we were making a promise—a vow that we would always remember where we came from.

"As children, we did everything together," I said. "The challenges and all the fun helped shape us."

Beau said, "And we'll always be proud of it." "We carry this place in our hearts wherever we go."

As the sun went down and the reflection of the orange bricks colored the atmosphere, we stood on the sidewalk and chatted for a bit. We could hear the sounds of music and laughter from neighbors gathered outdoors that surrounded us and rekindled the memories we had in that familiar place.

"Let's promise this place that we will be faithful and never forget our beginnings here," I vowed. "We must remember the lessons we have learned from our childhood growing up here."

"For life!" Beau then replied in a confident tone.

We kept talking, reminiscing about our days in the neighborhood that shaped us. KTown was more than a neighborhood project. It was part of our identity that we would never let go.

Insights from the Chapter: Kinship Beyond Blood

The feeling of coming home—not just physically but emotionally is therapeutic. The streets may have aged, but the spirit of the neighborhood remains unchanged, much like the bond between old friends.

Meeting Beau again felt like uncovering a piece of the past, a reminder that time may move forward, but some connections stay just as strong. What we conversed about was a testament to the values we were raised with—loyalty, respect, and the unspoken promise to always look out for each other. KTown wasn't just a place; it was a community that shaped us, taught us resilience, and instilled a deep sense of belonging.

The memory of childhood struggles, school fights, and the simple joy of 50-cent cinnamon rolls brings back a shared history that shaped our identities. But more than that, our exchange is a vow to carry KTown in our hearts no matter where life takes us.

The genuine joy of reconnection is not just about reminiscing—it's about reaffirming that the values and bonds that formed in our youth still hold weight. The sign language 'K' for KTown isn't just a gesture; it's a symbol of unbreakable loyalty.

As we stood on the sidewalk, surrounded by laughter and music, the message was clear: no matter how far we go, KTown will always be home.

Twenty-Six

A New Beginning in an Old Place

When I first ran into Beau, it felt like a throwback to another lifetime. An unexpected collision of past and present. I hadn't seen him in years. The last time we'd seen each other was right here, in the neighborhood that raised us— KTown. A lot had changed since then, both in the neighborhood and in us. We were two people returning to familiar territory that had become unfamiliar over time.

We had a lot to share with each other. As we stood together and caught up, we shared stories about where we had been and the challenges life had presented.

Beau had lived a life that seemed unimaginable to me, one marked by more than just survival — a story of resilience that I hadn't known he possessed. He shared pieces of his life, some of which were hard to hear. "The best but not the best of life," he called it, his eyes distant yet sharp. I could see the resilience in his face and feel it in his words. KTown hadn't been kind to many of us, but Beau's story struck me in ways I hadn't expected.

Beau was only a teenager, like me, when his brother was murdered. I remember hearing about it back then and the shock and grief it brought to the neighborhood. But I hadn't realized the weight of it for Beau until that moment when I finally heard his side of the story. He told me he'd lost his mind afterward, unable to cope with the pain. For a whole five years, he said, he didn't change his clothes, drifting from one abandoned house to another. He lived on the streets, lost to the world in a way that felt unfixable.

As he told me this, I looked at him with a kind of stunned amazement, realizing how close he'd come to disappearing entirely. In some ways, I'd already thought he might have. He'd always been somewhat of an outcast in KTown. So many kids like him didn't survive the trials that came their way. Many of the trouble-making kids never survived their rough childhood. The burden of their hardships caused some to be imprisoned, others to be slain, and yet others to just disappear. And yet here Beau was, breathing, still standing, and somehow navigating his way back from the precipice.

Beau told me that after his brother's death, he developed a mental illness, schizophrenia, and he became paranoid, especially toward the police. "If they shot at me, I shot back," he said bluntly, his voice heavy with memories. Those years, the pain and the anger had carved deep scars into him. But at some point, something unexpectedly changed. He'd come to his senses, as he put it, and managed to pull himself out of that dark place.

For a time, he found steady work as a truck driver, a job that took him far from KTown to dangerous places and around people who could be just as destructive. He told me, "Faithe, the money got me. I couldn't pass it up." I could see the temptation that had drawn him in and the consequences that followed. Eventually, he was caught, served his time in the Feds, and found himself right back here, where it had all started.

But suffering wasn't the only thing life had given him. From his incarceration, Beau had gained something unexpected: solitude. During those years, he read, learned, and–above all–became closer to God. He told me how his faith had been his compass and how he had found solace in the Bible.

For him, it was more than just words on paper; it was a chance to start again from scratch — a lifeline. His comments moved me, especially when I began reflecting on my own development as a Christian. My family had been devoted to our church when I was a child, but I had drifted away after it disbanded. I tried a few different churches, but none of them seemed to stick, so I soon stopped going to church completely. I hadn't set foot inside a church in seven years when I ran into Beau again.

Beau and I were supposed to be opposites — him, the one who'd taken a path of rebellion, and me, the "good girl." But it was him who helped lead me back to faith. After that day, we exchanged numbers, agreeing to keep in touch. When Beau called me a few days later, it seemed as though we had discovered something significantly new in one another. We started to have uplifting effects on one another.

Beau and I began hiking together, finding walking spots and gardens that took us away from the sad streets of KTown. We renewed a sacred part of ourselves when we started going to church together. Beau even decided to get baptized again, a symbolic act to reclaim his commitment to faith. KTown might have taken a downturn, with drugs creeping into corners that used to be safe and people struggling in ways they hadn't before. But somehow, in this place where we'd both been shaped and scarred, we found a sense of hope.

Being with my old friend Beau again seemed like a new beginning in an old environment. It served as a reminder that no matter where life took us, we could always go back–not just to a particular place but also to our identity and what we wanted from life. Finding a better way to live and overcome the hurt were the main goals of our reunion, not only going over the past.

Even though KTown might have been a difficult neighborhood to grow up in, I felt that coming back could help us rebuild — something I thought as Beau and I stood there. This old neighborhood, regardless of how scarred it was, still held memories of our innocence, friendships, and second chances.

Insights from the Chapter: Divine Timing and Redemption Through Return

My unexpected encounter with Beau wasn't just a mere coincidence. It was a path that God carved for me to lead me back to Him. This made me realize how He works in mysterious ways and guides us to where we are supposed to be at the right time.

K-Town, the old neighborhood where I grew up, has indeed become a difficult and dangerous place to be. But it is where I found myself again. It is the place that, once again, brings me closer to God.

After meeting Beau, I healed wounds I never even knew needed healing. He and I both restarted our lives in a place we never thought we would return to.

In the end, we found our way back to a place that we once missed. This gives me the insight that sometimes, old places can become new beginnings.

Twenty-Seven

Stolen Lives

I still remember the night it happened, the night everything changed. It was quiet—almost too quiet, almost eerily so. And then, just like that, news shot through the neighborhood that my brother was gone. Dead over twenty dollars. Twenty dollars. You'd think it was a sick joke, something you'd hear in a bad movie. But it was real. They'd shot him in the neck, right there, over a couple of crumpled bills that wouldn't even cover a day's worth of food.

After that night, KTown wasn't the same. I wasn't the same. We all felt like something had been ripped out of us. He wasn't just my brother; he was part of our community, part of all of us. He was the guy everyone respected, the one who could make a bad day feel better with just a nod or a joke. He looked out for everyone; it didn't matter who. And he'd always looked out for me. Then, in the blink of an eye, he was gone.

I didn't know what to do with the pain. It was like nothing I'd felt before—like losing a limb. I thought I could hold it together at first, but it just kept eating at me. Every day felt like I was waking up in a nightmare I couldn't shake. I'd walk around, and go to places we used to hang out, and he was nowhere. Just… gone. A hole where he'd been.

For a long time, I couldn't face people. I stopped changing clothes and stopped caring about anything. I drifted through abandoned houses and slept wherever I could find a spot. I was numb, but the hurt was still there, buried under everything, a dull throb reminding me that he was gone. People must've thought I was crazy, but I didn't care. I was lost in my own world, a world that didn't make sense without him in it.

The police saw me as trouble like I was some kind of threat. And I guess, in some ways, I was. I hated them. I was paranoid. Every time they came near me, I felt like they were out to get me, like they'd taken something that belonged to me. The anger burned so hot; there were times I just wanted them to feel the pain I was carrying around every day.

But then, eventually, the fog lifted, at least a little. I was still angry, still broken, but I found a way to survive. I started driving trucks, got out of KTown, and met people I'd never have met otherwise. I got mixed up in dangerous stuff, sure. Made choices I wouldn't make today. But back then, the money was good, and I needed something to fill the emptiness. It was like a high—a distraction from all the darkness I couldn't escape.

Then I got caught and spent some time in the Feds. It was there, sitting alone in those cells, that I realized I couldn't keep going down the same path. I started reading, praying, even praying, and for the first time, I felt like there might be a way out of the hole I'd dug for myself.

I learned that forgiveness is real and that maybe my brother would've wanted me to live, really live, instead of wasting away. It was a strange thought, and I didn't fully believe it right away. But it stuck with me. And when I got out, I came back to KTown—not to stay, but to remember where I came from. To face what I'd been running from.

And that's when I ran into you again. I didn't think anyone from those days would still be around, but there you were, and it felt like maybe things could be different. Maybe the weight of my brother's death didn't have to crush me forever. Maybe there was a way to hold his memory without letting it destroy me.

I'm still haunted, don't get me wrong. The scars don't go away. But I'm trying, and that's something I couldn't say back then.

Insights from the Chapter: Brokenness, Belief, and Becoming

Losing my brother was the deepest wound I've ever experienced. But through the pain, I learned that grief can either bury you or become the soil where something new grows.

God didn't take away my suffering, but He stayed with me through it. Even in the numbness and the nights spent in abandoned places, He was quietly working, waiting for me to turn toward Him.

KTown, once a place filled with heartbreak and anger, became the ground for healing. Going back wasn't about returning to the past. It was about facing it and finding purpose in it.

The prison cell I feared became a place of awakening. In the silence, I finally began to hear God's voice. That's when I started to believe forgiveness wasn't just for others. It was for me, too.

Pain doesn't disappear easily, and neither do the scars. But I've come to see that trying, even while broken, is a powerful act of faith.

In the end, I realized that the hardest roads often lead us right where we're meant to be. Not because we planned it but because God never stopped guiding us.

Twenty-Eight

Roads Not Taken

Beau started telling me stories that delved into the depths of what he had been through as we spent more time together. The more he shared, the more I realized just how close to the edge he had lived and how life had tried again and again to pull him under. But Beau seemed to have a certain resilience that kept him going, even in the darkest moments.

One day, he shared a memory that still felt raw. He was only twenty-one, just a young man, still in KTown. He'd been walking down the hill near where I grew up, on a street so familiar that every crack in the pavement, every rusting mailbox felt like home. He was just walking, maybe heading somewhere, or maybe nowhere at all, just lost in his own thoughts. But that didn't matter to whoever was in the car. That slowed as it approached. Beau's back was turned, and he didn't see it coming.

"They just started shooting," he said, his voice low. "I didn't even know I'd been hit at first, didn't feel it, but I fell. Felt the ground more than the bullets. I was shot 10 times. Next thing I knew, I was on the pavement, looking up at the sky."

The shooter wasn't even after him, he told me, just mistook him for someone else. Beau was paralyzed from the waist down and on the verge of death due to a horrible turn of events. He lay in a hospital bed for months, staring at the ceiling, not knowing if he would ever be able to walk again. For someone like Beau, who had always been active, risky, and proud, it felt like a cage. All he could do was wait and pray while his entire world shrank into those four walls.

His brother, the one who'd always been his protector, had stayed by his side as much as he could. Beau told me about one day in particular when they'd been in the middle of an argument, frustration and fear getting the best of them both. His brother, in a moment of anger, had grabbed him to move him, lifting him roughly. Beau fell forward, his body bracing against his own resistance, and in that strange moment, he felt something shift inside.

"It was like a light coming back on," he said. My body seemed to recall what I was meant to accomplish. I began to feel once more. His nerves had been stimulated back into activity somehow by that tumble to the ground. Beau was able to walk again after some time, consistent therapy, and rehabilitation. It was nothing less than a miracle for him.

He looked at me, a small, almost shy smile breaking across his face. "I don't know what to call it other than God. I think He's kept me here for a reason, kept me from leaving this world when I should've been gone."

As we sat on that porch in KTown, I could see Beau reliving those moments, the pain, the helplessness, and the gratitude that had replaced them. He told me about the times he'd died, his heart stopping twice after the shooting. "I saw something," he said, his voice softer now, "something that can't be explained. It was like... I was being shown that there was more for me to do. That I wasn't done yet."

When he came back to life, he said he'd felt changed, somehow different. Suddenly, the words of the Bible, which he'd grown up hearing but never really understood, came alive to him. He could read it, and it made sense in a way it never had before. When things didn't make sense in his life, it served as a guide and a lifeline.

As I listened to him, I understood that despite Beau's life's attempts to shatter him in every manner conceivable–through physical suffering, sadness, and gunshot wounds–something inside of him had resisted. He gave God the credit for his life, the odd experiences that saved him from certain death, and the opportunity to walk again. As I sat beside him, watching the people pass by, it hit me just how much strength it took for Beau to have made it this far.

KTown wasn't the same place we'd grown up in. The streets had changed. People had moved on or passed away. But it was also the place where Beau got into trouble, where early wounds taught him, in a strange way, how to survive. We were back in the neighborhood where our childhood connected us, reviewing the past and trying to find methods to mend old wounds despite everything that had happened. Beau's is an example of perseverance and a reminder that while life is never simple, sometimes the most difficult paths lead us to our true selves.

Insights from the Chapter: Still Breathing, Still Becoming

Listening to Beau's story reminded me that some of the most powerful testimonies come from the places we least expect. His life, shaped by trauma, loss, and the brink of death, also reflects incredible resilience and grace. What stood out most was how God didn't remove the pain but used it to stir something deeper in him—a quiet transformation that began in the midst of suffering.

There are times when life feels like it's closing in, when hope fades, and the future looks impossible. Beau had lived through more than one of those moments. Shot ten times, paralyzed, and clinically dead, he still came back. Each experience wasn't just survival. It was a message that he still had more to do, more to give. His recovery wasn't just physical. It was spiritual. He began to see the Bible in a new light. Words that once meant nothing now guided him.

What I learned is that miracles often happen in silence. Not with flashes of light, but in quiet hospital rooms, in long days of waiting, in moments of surrender. Beau's healing didn't come all at once but through time, struggle, and faith. And through all of it, he recognized that it was God who had carried him through.

This reminded me that even in our darkest hours, purpose can be found. God does not waste pain. Sometimes, what looks like the end is actually the beginning of something we never imagined.

Book Blurb

Resilience, loyalty, sorrow, and redemption are all depicted in this collection of events in the neighborhood known as KTown, a place that challenged and became a part of those who lived there. The characters' journey demonstrates that the ultimate strength to live and thrive comes from the support of others and the advice of friends rather than from within, through times of childhood innocence, tragedies, terrible loss, and personal growth.

The journey begins with friendships in the shared experiences of childhood, forming an unbreakable bond. Loyalty, respect, and the promise to never forget one's roots create the narrative, grounding the characters in a shared sense of identity. As the story unfolds, memories lead to a deeper understanding of oneself and the powerful role that family and home surroundings play in shaping our identity.

These chapters tell the story of a community where hardship and hope collide. The experiences from the past guide the way forward. This book displays the transformational power of friendship. The stories of the characters serve as a reminder that friends can guide us toward recovery, rejuvenation, and a purposeful life to bring us from our worst moments.

Made in the USA
Las Vegas, NV
03 September 2025

27324791R00083